*A Garland Series*

# OUTSTANDING
# DISSERTATIONS
# IN THE

# FINE
# ARTS

# Hellenistic Statues of Aphrodite

## Studies in the History of their Stylistic Development

Dericksen Morgan Brinkerhoff

*Garland Publishing, Inc., New York and London*

*1978*

All volumes in this series are printed
on acid-free, 250-year-life paper.

Library of Congress Cataloging in Publication Data

Brinkerhoff, Dericksen M
    Hellenistic statues of Aphrodite.

    (Outstanding dissertations in the fine arts)
    Originally presented as the author's thesis,
Harvard, 1958.
    Bibliography:  p.
    1.  Venus (Goddess)--Art.  2.  Sculpture,
Hellenistic.  I.  Title.  II.  Series.
NB163.V5B74  1978          731'.88'92211     77-94688
ISBN 0-8240-3217-9

Printed in the United States of America

The honor of inclusion in the distinguished Garland series must be tempered with a reminder to the reader that the following example of youthful scholarship is now two decades old. The persistent paucity of externally datable monuments has continued to challenge those who would better comprehend the sculpture of the Hellenistic era. Those studies that bear most directly upon the evidence accepted in the dissertation and on its discussion of stylistic concepts warrant citation here.

Andreas Linfert, in "Der Meister der kauernden Aphrodite," AM 84 (1969) 158-164, has scrutinized and rejected persuasively the long accepted emendation of Pliny the Elder reviewed below in chapter two. In doing so, he reduced the presumed existence of the master Doidalsas to fantasy, deleted one of the few chronological anchors from the art of the third century B.C., and severed the conventional connection of Polycharmos with the Aphrodite binding her sandal, cited here in chapter four. My reassessment, expanding on the subject of chapter two, will appear under the title, "Hypotheses on the History of the Crouching Aphrodite Type in Antiquity," in the J. Paul Getty Museum Journal in 1978. It proposes advancing the date of the Hellenistic creation to the end of the third century, and endeavors to explain the relationship of the motif to the classical past. In a similar vein, Brunilde S. Ridgway would relocate in the second century one of the works compared here with

the sandalbinding Aphrodite in her essay, "The Date of the so-called
Lysippean Jason," AJA 68 (1964) 113-128, dissertation illustration
Pl. XIX. Her conclusion tends to support one of the premises of this
dissertation, that considerable activity characterized the second
century, and that its art generally bears a conscious relation to the
past. Yet our perceptions of which work preceded and which followed in
sculptural sequences needs constant reexamination. A reversal of my own
opinion expressed in chapter five below resulted from a second look at
the Capitoline Aphrodite, my navel analysis notwithstanding, so that I
would now place that statue in the fourth century, and the Medici
Aphrodite in the second. See, "Figures of Venus, Creative and Deri-
vative," in Studies Presented to George M. A. Hanfmann, eds. D. G.
Mitten, J. G. Pedley, and J. A. Scott ("Fogg Art Museum, Harvard
University Monographs in Art and Archaeology," II; Cambridge 1971) 9-16.
Ridgway, in another discussion, "The Aphrodite of Arles," AJA 80 (1976)
147-154, gives her hypothesis on the sequence of Hellenistic statues of
Aphrodite. Her proposal to disassociate from Praxiteles the Arles
figure, and to see it as a creation of the Augustan age, recalling
Furtwängler's bold disaffiliation from the same master of the Aphrodite
of Melos, is worthy of close study in the presence of the statue. The
recent years of Hellenistic scholarship seem replete with efforts to
advance the dates of the works examined. P. H. von Blanckenhagen's
removal of the already peripatetic Laocoon, "Laokoon, Sperlonga und
Vergil," AA (1969) 256-75, stimulated by discoveries now examined and
published by B. Conticello and B. Andreae, "Die Skulpturen von Sperlonga,"

<u>Antike Plastik</u> 14 (1974), has surely provided the most dramatic and extreme example.

Any future broad investigation of figures and concepts of Aphrodite will benefit from the evidence collected by Achille Adriani in his <u>Repertorio d'arte dell'Egitto greco-romano</u>, <u>Serie</u> A, I- (Palermo 1961-date). The same applies to the careful study by Gloria S. Merker, <u>The Hellenistic Sculpture of Rhodes</u> ("Studies in Mediterranean Archaeology," XL; Göteborg 1973). Finally, any general treatment appraising Hellenistic schemata for the depiction of the human figure can derive support from the solid evidence garnered painstakingly by Dorothy Burr Thompson in her <u>Ptolemaic Oinochoai and Portraits in Faience: Aspects of the Ruler-Cult</u> ("Oxford Monographs on Classical Archaeology"; Oxford 1973).

The text of the present edition has been prepared by Marilyn Asbell in elite type. The consequent reduction in number of pages compared to the original text in pica typescript has meant a mismatch in the pagination, but has also resulted in a minimum price for the published version. Mary Brinkerhoff, my ever helpful wife, Catherine Lees-Causey and the author shared the procfreading, the last eschewing temptations, all too numerous, to alter the text.

Any one investigating the statue of the Crouching Aphrodite who wishes to coordinate the numismatic evidence should rely on a geography of classical Anatolia, for my references, as Professor T. R. S. Broughton pointed out to me, are confused. The figure of the Aphrodite Anadyomene illustrated on Pl. XLVIII and cited as "Coll. Wright, on Loan to the University Museum, Philadelphia," now belongs to the museum.  I

owe this information to Professor Ridgway, who also informs me that

the statue and the anadyomene type formed the subject of an as yet

unpublished fine M.A. thesis at Bryn Mawr College by Nancy Winter,

currently librarian of the American School of Classical Studies in

Athens.  It is good to know in presenting this dissertation to a wider

public that others find the subject it pursues a rewarding avenue for

investigation.


                                                        D. M. B.
                                                        Riverside,
February, 1978                                          California

Hellenistic Statues of Aphrodite:   Studies in the History

of their Stylistic Development


A thesis presented

by

Dericksen Morgan Brinkerhoff

to

The Department of Fine Arts

in partial fulfillment of the requirements

for the degree of

Doctor of Philosophy

in the subject of

History and Principles of Fine Arts


Harvard University

Cambridge, Massachusetts

April, 1958

ACKNOWLEDGEMENTS

For assistance in bringing this study to its present state, I wish to thank the following. First, gratitude must be expressed to Professor George M. A. Hanfmann for aid beyond the call of duty as my thesis advisor. Next, I want to state my appreciation for helpful comment and criticism concerning the present whereabouts of some of the statues discussed to Dr. Cornelius C. Vermeule, Jr., Curator of the Classical Collection at the Museum of Fine Arts, Boston. Dr. Hazel Palmer, the Assistant Curator, has called my attention to a number of the most recent and also several little known publications relevant to this field. Professors Evelyn Harrison and Dorothy Thompson, and Dr. Dorothy K. Hill, who grace Colombia University, The Institute for Advanced Study, and the Walters Art Gallery, respectively, have contributed advice and constructive criticism. For assistance in obtaining photographs I am indebted to the staffs of the various museums, societies, and other institutions cited. Thanks should also go to Miss Katherine Austin, Mr. Robert Thornton, Photographer at Rhode Island School of Design, and to my wife, who helped prepare the illustrations. Miss Norma Moore typed the manuscript.

TABLE OF CONTENTS

LIST OF PLATES

HELLENISTIC STATUES OF APHRODITE:   STUDIES IN THE

HISTORY OF THEIR STYLISTIC DEVELOPMENT

CHAPTER I

INTRODUCTION

Hellenistic art, more important and less understood than that of
any other period in the civilization of ancient Greece, influenced
visual expression in the Western world for two thousand years, and in
the East for one thousand. Its sculpture is clearly Greek, yet its
images, spirit and centers of production are each broader in their
range and different in their character from the works of the classic
age. The term Hellenistic, meaning Greeklike, defines a natural
division in the political history of the Eastern Mediterranean area
from the reign of Alexander the Great, 336-323 B.C., to the supremacy
of Rome and Augustus after the battle of Actium in 30 B.C. The artistic
products of this age constituted a bridge linking the Greek era with the
Roman, and as Greek artists came under Hellenized Roman patronage, they
copied and adapted older works already created, lending credence to the
theories that Roman art is really Greek.[1] Since many of the features
usually associated with Roman art can be traced to Hellenistic
beginnings, the earlier period may also be looked upon as a prelude to
the later one. Is it not preferable to go beyond the mere, even trite,
observation that the apparent sunset of one age is but the dawn of
another, and examine Hellenistic art in its own right?

This study attempts to bring about a clearer perspective of one of the most significant aspects of the period for modern man. It is concerned with its stylistic evolution as evident in the creation and development of the most outstanding plastic representations of the goddess Aphrodite. The subject of the female figure, relatively naturalistically depicted in a nude or half-draped state, commenced its long career in the history of Western art at this time. The types established during the second half of the fourth century B.C. led to others in the third, and all were elaborated upon toward the end of the Hellenistic era.

The repertoire thus formed crystallized under the hegemony of Roman patronage. Various Hellenistic versions of the goddess, known through numerous examples, have become so well known that they have constituted the stock in trade of Western artists dealing with this theme ever since, with the exception of the Medieval epoch. Scarcely any depiction in sculpture or painting of the female nude is without its debt, tacit or explicit, to the pioneering experimenters of the Hellenistic centuries. Yet the origins of these figures have remained stubbornly obscure and their makers, with few exceptions persistently shadowlike, have clung to a haunting limbo seemingly inaccessible to modern eyes and minds. The goal of this examination then is not to add to the acclaim some of the statues have already received, but to insert them into their proper places as prime and revealing specimens of the sculpture of the Hellenistic age. Such labors may help to delineate more accurately the true dimensions of the past in this particular area of human endeavor.

The causes of previous difficulties in ordering and explaining these creations of Aphrodite are not in the least elusive. At the root of the matter lie our own conflicting theories of Hellenistic sculpture, matching and mismatching evidence unearthed through all the apparatus of recent scholarship relative to the fields of history and its cognates archaeology, philology, the history of religion, and of art. Compounding the confusion are the quantity, variety, and differing types of original statues and copies surviving from antiquity, as large as life or small enough to fit on the head of a pin, existing in one unique version or over a hundred of the most disparate quality. Their study is, of course, often subject to well intentioned but frequently obfuscatory restorations, true also of the entire field of Greek sculpture.

Finally, one must point out that, where copies of originals are concerned, it is necessary to distinguish between those characteristics contributed by the copyist, who may or may not have been attempting to imitate the original literally, and those associated with its first creation. For these reasons it is essential to preface this investigation with an account of Hellenistic sculpture in general, followed by a discussion of the representations of Aphrodite in particular.

1. Evaluations of Hellenistic Sculpture

Previous reactions to the sculpture of this era have seen in it bewildering confusion, and often a loss of creative vitality. Interpretations have explained its variety by positing local schools, and have measured its development against cyclic laws. The unit normally understood as the Hellenistic period is a large one. It is as long in extent of time as were the earlier archaic, and entire classic ages until the time of Alexander. The art of this three-century span can obviously be distinguished from that of the preceding era by a number of factors, the most important of which are the sudden geographical diversification in connection with the Hellenistic kingdoms and the stylistic multiplicity of manner and subject. One's first impression is that these differences are overwhelming in contrast to the coherent consistency of the years between 600 and 300 B.C., a reaction substantiated by the following quotation from Bieber:[2]

"Following the conquest of new countries by Alexander and his successors, new realms were also conquered for art...

As a consequence, the greatest peculiarity of this period is the great variety of styles which evolved in response to these many new tasks. The Hellenistic artists replaced the ideals of the classical period -- serenity, harmony, and balance -- with stormy passion, sincere realism, contrast of softest sweetness and distorted ugliness, violence of movement, figures crowded together in space or relieved against a rich background. To all

of these, peculiar to Hellenistic art, was added an occasional
return to earlier styles."

In short, Hellenistic sculpture can not be approached in a manner
consonant with the study of the art of the previous ages.  So bewildering
has the later era appeared to be with its absence of simplicity, lack of
a limited variety of grand themes, and repetition of earlier ones that
it has also been looked upon as a period of decadence.  Such a conclusion
is partly based upon the feeling that during this time the "occasional
return to earlier styles" and the deliberate archaism which later
developed into the neo-Attic art of the first centuries B.C. and A.D.
under Roman patronage are evidence of a loss of creativity, a reaction
sometimes supported by pointing to the frequent wars among the kingdoms
and the intermittent but increasing loss of independence to Rome.  Such
criticism can employ a quantitative fallacy, by pointing to the vast
array of mediocre work, surviving largely through copies, in the
galleries and cellars of our museums.

That a citation of the conclusion that Hellenistic art is more
properly a field for the pathologist is no idle digression is attested
to by the following three quotations.  First comes the opinion of Clive
Bell, who wrote during the excitement of the early twentieth century's
discovery of "pure form," Cézanne, Gauguin, Van Gogh, and cubism.[3]
"From the heights of primitive form, art declined with the Greeks to
peter out in the bogs of Hellenistic and Roman rubbish."  From this
condemnation of any art but archaic, estimations of the classic period

easily recovered, but many have continued to hold the succeeding age in
disrepute. Witness the Oxford Classical Dictionary.[4] "Apart from
portraiture Hellenistic sculpture was mainly an experiment in pastiches,
with a permanent tendency to be synthetic rather than original. Few
outstanding works are preserved, but the Victory of Samothrace and the
sculpture in high relief from the Altar of the Gods at Pergamon show
respectively a revival of fifth-century style and a new experiment in
baroque, the first of its kind in Greece." The grudging admission that
a limited quantity of Hellenistic work can be considered original is
not, however, typical of certain scholars of indubitable distinction
such as Sir Kenneth Clark, whose brilliant analyses of conceptions
original to Hellenistic artists includes the comment, "but it is
remarkable that in the female nude there is hardly a single idea of
lasting value that was not originally discovered in the fourth century."[5]
It might be added that Sir Kenneth is convinced that the type of the
crouching Aphrodite was a certain product of the early fourth century
B.C., in spite of his awareness of its attribution to Doidalsas around
250 B.C.[6] While allowance must always be made for personal taste, the
studies in the successive chapters of this investigation will, it is
hoped, reveal that while the problem of creative originality in the
Hellenistic period is a very real one, its art, viewed on its own
merits, possesses genuine esthetic value.

The advent of Miss Bieber's Sculpture of the Hellenistic Age in New
York in 1955, an archaeological study of the first magnitude, prompted
one authority of note to append to his review of the book a proposed

account of the evolution of Hellenistic sculpture in stylistic terms.[7]
In the course of his discussion of the challenge of its meager dated
evidence he delineated the problem with succinct clarity:[8]

"The scaffolding for Hellenistic sculptural chronology had
therefore to be constructed somehow from within. But it was not
clear how this could be done, precisely because Hellenistic
sculpture was no longer 'classic,' in the sense that it seemed
emancipated from that long process of technical formal evolution
which had dictated to all earlier sculpture a discoverable place
and determinable function in the development from archaism to
objective realism. If the ability to reproduce fully and without
arbitrary convention the natural shapes of the physical world...
had at last been attained during the lifetime of the Lysippic
school, must it not follow that the subsequent behavior of
sculptural art would have been subject to no more discoverable law
than the changing moods of fashion and the personal talent of the
artists?"

One should assess the previous efforts to overcome this troublesome
absence of predictability in contrast to archaic and classic art, either
by assigning examples of Hellenistic sculpture to various schools, or by
endeavoring to discover and define the operation of a law of polarity,
to associate datable works with others by period. Concerning the former,
mention should be made here of the carefully considered conclusions of
Miss Richter, presented in her <u>Three Critical Periods in Greek Sculpture</u>.[9]
There she discussed evidence, as did Carpenter, to support the contention

that the idea of separate schools is a misnomer if understood literally, for she showed how many of the artists, at Pergamon for example, were drawn to centers far distant from their homelands.[10] Laboring for specific patrons, and often under the guidance of a particular artist, they tended to work in a well-defined manner, and probably continued to produce sculpture of the same style in other places at a later time. Besides the characteristic fusion of passion and naturalism for dramatic purposes which distinguished a piece as Pergamene in spirit if not in fact, there was a delicate **sfumato** style, once identified as Alexandrian, but now recognized as a more widespread, post-Praxitelean technique.

In the face of this evidence for a cosmopolitan unity, a **koiné**, it should not be forgotten that if an example of a particular manner be proven to be typical for a single area at a specific time, then it is still most accurate to label a distinctive style as characteristic of and emanating from a certain center. This may seem like eating one's cake and having it too, yet the older, conventional grouping into schools retains a measure of sense if it be understood in the same way that terms like Attic and Ionian hold good as stylistic labels for earlier Greek sculpture. That is to say, far from being uniquely and bafflingly different, the same relative diversity and unity, helpful in distinguishing the phases of archaic and classic art, are true of Hellenistic, and in this respect the latter period merely continued the overall makeup characteristic of Greek art. Regional preferences often shaped by a dominant artistic personality within the inclusive framework of Greek style distinguish both the classic and the Hellenistic ages in sculpture. Yet, in terms of stating clearly how that style developed

through centuries, neither schools nor the expressions Pheidian or post-

Praxitelean suffice to explain the breadth of the artistic chronological

development of any Greek age.

The other attempt to render clarity out of apparent complexity has

been the assignment of rhythmic phases to the years 330-30 B.C. in a

kind of alternating polarity. Such a dangerously deterministic approach

can, if employed with cautious reserve, be immensely illuminating, but

its deceptively simple deductions must be inclined to disregard certain

artistic forms and overemphasize others, if they are to convince. Yet

this system has been the only one to meet with a measure of lasting

success, but Carpenter, who lists its principal exponents, as well as

the fact that its external authority is self-imposed, appears to

reject it.[11]

The application of the concept of a regular waxing and waning of

specific traits within the history of art understood as the development

of style to Hellenistic has demonstrated another characteristic device

by which it may be rendered comprehensible and predictable. The most

suggestive but least successful was the attempt by Wilhelm Klein to

apply literally the Baroque-Rococo sequence of later European art to

the third and second centuries B.C. in which Hellenistic Rococo was

understood as a certain gaiety of spirit, a deliberate choice of

Dionysiac subject, and the triumph of the decorative instinct over the

formal.[12] It appeared less dexterous when a convincing sequence of

examples was attempted, for Klein's collection was composed primarily
of small statuettes or terra-cotta miniatures, as Carpenter points out.
These featured the very types and motifs one might expect to emphasize
a deliberate and artful charm for its own sake, but they began clearly
with the incipient humanization of divinity and the livelier mythological figures of the late classic and early Hellenistic periods by
Praxiteles and Lysippus, and other masters.  It is not possible here to
consider further what was or was not valid in the seductive idea of an
ancient rococo.

A more fundamental and fruitful approach, because it appraised the
third, second, and first centuries more on their own terms, was that of
Krahmer, who worked out and tested his understanding of the age in a
series of groundbreaking essays in the 1920's which all succeeding
investigations have taken into account.[13]  His classification divided
the Hellenistic era into three periods.  The first, extending from 300
(-280) B.C. to 240(-225) B.C., tended to produce works in a simple,
straightforward style, whose compositions were centripetal and turned
back upon themselves.  The second period emerged from the first at the
time of the first Attalid dedication, the so-called large Gauls, and
included the Pergamene figures.  Its style he labelled pompous or even
pathetic, and its compositions radiate into space.  This diffusion of
energy led to a weaker but agitated classicizing phase after 150 B.C.
It may be summarily stated as:

1. Early Hellenistic period      330-225 B.C. closed form.

2. Middle Hellenistic period      225-150 B.C. open form.

3. Late Hellenistic period      150-75 B.C. classicistic.

To these Krahmer appended the first century B.C. which one might define as:

4. Graeco-Roman period, 75-_4 B.C., reminiscences of open form.

It is at this point that the writer diverges from Carpenter, for he states of Krahmer's centripetal and centrifugal:[14]

> "There can be no doubt that such a distinction exists,
> though it may be doubted whether as a system of stylistic
> classification it is anything more profound than a convenience
> of descriptive terms. At least, if the Dancing Faun and the
> Seated Hermes from the Vesuvian towns copy early third century
> bronzes of the post-Lysippan school and the hunched-up marble
> Poseidippos of the Vatican derives from the same period, it is
> demonstrably possible for centrifugal and centripetal compositions
> to co-exist as exact contemporaries."

Such a statement is not an accurate reflection of the thesis of Krahmer, who maintained that different types of compositions could co-exist, but that within the Hellenistic age there was a steadily increasing emphasis upon open form during the third century B.C., which became dominant by the time of the Middle Hellenistic period, just as the classicistic tendencies prevalent in the second century before Christ were not entirely absent during the earlier phases.[15] In

Carpenter's citation of the Dancing Faun and Seated Hermes there is
another weakness, for it is more reasonable to suppose that these belong
to the Late Hellenistic years, and are only inspired by immediate post-
Lysippic works, which they do not imitate literally, coming as they do
from Pompeii and Herculaneum. Certainly their contrived grace is more
appropriate to a later Hellenistic date, and this likelihood is
reinforced by recalling the original Crouching Aphrodite's composition,
and what became of it 150 years later, by the end of the second century
B.C. when the Rhodian variant demonstrated how a centripetal composition
could be handled in a centrifugal fashion (Pl. XII cf. Pl. XIII).[16]

In fact, Carpenter's account of the evolution of Hellenistic
sculpture, on rereading, becomes both more stimulating and more suspect.
It would be well to present a slightly different account here, against
which the former one might be placed.

2. An Analysis of the Development of Hellenistic Sculpture

The heritage of the fourth century B.C. consisted of an artistic
vocabulary of forms and subjects dominated by a new restlessness, which
may have been in part a reflection in art of political uncertainties.
It was also the result of the fact that the greater masters had
bequeathed to their successors new foundations for the further conquest
of physical reality and the depiction of mental states. Consequently,
the absorption in the representation of movement in space, detailed
observation guided by nature or specific characterization of impassioned,
or indrawn, or irresolute individuals, and occasional deliberate

archaisms testify that the Hellenistic centuries are no more and no less than the logical, but not inevitable, fulfillment of the previous centuries of Greek art. The early twentieth century's rapt admiration of archaic and classic has tended to set apart the final testimony of the Greek artistic genius, whose lavishing of technical skill on new plastic effects and unfamiliar subjects bewildered those who, ensnared by the biological or the moral fallacy, dismissed it as decadent.

Yet the pathos we associate with Scopas underlies the sympathetic approach to Greek philosophers or Gaulish warriors. The rich Hellenistic interpretations of drapery continue the experiments of many nameless or little known masters of the fourth century B.C. The richest fountainheads of invention, however, were undoubtedly Praxiteles and Lysippos. From the former's off-center poses, often incorporated with a support and perhaps a bemused interest in a lizard or the infant Dionysus, developed new bodily attitudes, and with his Aphrodite of Cnidos, a specific concentration, to be developed outwardly toward the spectator, or inward toward a new self-absorption. From the latter, who was really the first Hellenistic sculptor, sprang not only a new canon of human proportions, crossed or criss-crossed arms, legs and lines of drapery, but with a three-dimensional comprehension of form. With these men there commenced the dynamic analysis of the human figure conceived as solid rather than as plane geometry and as energy rather than mass, to culminate in the great friezes of the altar at Pergamon early in the second century B.C. Thus the idea of a break between the classic and the Hellenistic eras is a figment of the modern mind.

The early Hellenistic period is one whose primary interest lay in new poses, whose principal new subject is the monumental nude Aphrodite. The secondary focus of attention concerned naturalistic surfaces, and the luminous Praxitelean finish became a sfumato, while the taut skin treatment of Lysippus became a formula for athletic musculature. The result of this double concentration was to reinforce the growing tension between the figure and the surrounding space, seen already in the late Attic grave reliefs, stiff, isolated shapes projected before unyielding backgrounds. The contrived variety of the Tyche of Antioch, or the rigid separateness of the Demosthenes of Polyeuctos on whom are hung head, hands, and a veritable blanket of drapery show that the climax of this phase was reached by 280 B.C.[17] During the middle years of the third century before Christ, the progressive spatial isolation of the figure and the acquired habit of abstracting it into triangular and pyramidal shapes, tempered by accurate observation of nature, produced a masterpiece of closed form, the crouching Aphrodite of Doidalsas (Pls. IX, X, XIII). It was followed by the creation of the girl from Anzio, the "epithyousa" of Phanis, a pupil of Lysippus, about 240 B.C.,[18] in which elements of open and closed form can both be seen, in the effective contrasts between body and drapery, capped by the rapt, completely withdrawn psychological expression. To this large-headed, stocky and massive pair should be added the first of the heroic warrior groups, which may well be the "Pasquino," with Menelaus lifting the dead Patroclus.[19] These three examples reveal the initiation of a new phase, characterized by monumentality, formal inventiveness, and vigor, datable roughly to the third quarter of the third century before our era.

The naturalism evident in the weighty, pear-shaped body of the crouching Aphrodite, or the drooping lifelessness of Patroclus, reveals that, having achieved a mastery of pose, the primary fascination of this period was found in the close observation of nature. The products of these decades are not studies in repose, for the first of the Attalid dedications, the so-called large Gauls, have a manifold character. Combined with an increased emphasis on technique to recreate physical reality more precisely went the inclusion of ethnic types new to the Greek repertoire, sympathetically observed, as if the identity of mankind were stronger than the racial divisions separating its parts. One might suppose that Alexander the Great's dream of unity was echoed here, for, in Alexandria, negroes and other types found in the cosmopolitan Hellenistic cities were now interpreted with new awareness and understanding. Against a background of relative political stability one can discern more unity than diversity, as the same desire for accurate representation appeared within a broader choice of subject, which may be studied also in the strikingly handsome ruler portraits of the time on coins or through the imperfect echoes of copyist work in bronze and marble, except for a few notable originals.[20] This international style was everywhere characterized by the first stirrings from within, formally and psychologically, visible in both statues and groups, by a progressive opening and energizing of form, forecasting the imminent end of the centripetal straightforward, basic design axiom of the first three quarters of the third century B.C. Its richness and variety is nowhere better seen than in the group of Apollo, Marsyas and the Scythian knife grinder, three heterogeneous figures comprising an extraordinarily dramatic, spatially complex and psychologically involved unit.[21]

Into this period Carpenter would inject a quite fabulous collection of works.[22] In his own words, the period was "an undramatically naturalistic phase," for, "precisely because it studies nature so closely and reproduces it so carefully, the sculpture of the second half of the third century B.C. seems almost disappointingly featureless in its serenity." One can only agree with his perceptive understanding of the period prior to the advent of the first Gallic and Marsyas groups when he delimits it by stating:

"In any event it greatly belies Pliny's abrupt cessavit deinde ars (which may have referred merely to the great Sicyonian bronze foundry, whose Xenokrates he had been utilizing as a source of information). We should at least understand it well enough to see that it is out of its indrawn poses and direct observation of nature that the crouching Aphrodite of Doidalsas was created, and that by its devotion to anatomical truth the fifth century pedimental theme of the collapsing warrior was converted into the Dying Trumpeter of the Capitoline, who ushers in the next phase of Hellenistic sculpture with its renewed stirring of the craftsman's desire to call attention to his skill."

Carpenter would place in this period the originals of <u>Aphrodite</u> of
<u>Cyrene</u>, and of the <u>Praying Boy</u> in Berlin, the "Boston bronze head of the
third Arsinoë," and the marble <u>Boy</u> from Perinthos, in Athens, the bronze
portrait of <u>Arsinoë III</u> in Mantua, and the echoes of portraits seen from
coins showing Berenice II and Philistis of Syracuse. Of this phase he
states, "They constitute the least studied and most poorly understood
chapter in Greek sculptural history." Truer words were never penned,
for two of those first cited above have been transported back and forth
across the Hellenistic centuries for fifty years; one is a problem piece
and one doesn't even exist. The Cyrene Aphrodite (Pls. XLIII-IV) to
Carpenter, "expertly copied in late imperial Roman times from a Hellenistic bronze of the third quarter of the third century B.C. embodies
and displays in exquisite perfection the deceptive simplicity of pose,
subtlety of surface and nonchalant ease of volume, which characterize
this phase of unexaggerated Naturalism." This may be a correct and
discriminating guess with which the writer agrees, but its striking
resemblance to the anatomical construction and outline of the Aphrodite
of Melos now dated c. 100 B.C., or to the same goddess in the qualita-
tively poorer "pantoufle" group of Aphrodite and Pan from Delos reinforce the present attribution of the Cyrene statue, as an adaptation,
to the turn of the first century B.C., contrary to Carpenter's late
Roman imperial date.[23] The Praying Boy, which Carpenter feels "is
almost a companion piece to the Aphrodite" seems so because its similar
smoothness of surface and artificial, posed quality link it closely to
the revival of Lysippic figures for use as Roman garden decoration,

along with the dancing faun and seated Hermes.[24] Turning to the "Boston
bronze" of Arsinoë III, it appears that this was either a confused
reference to the bronze head sometimes identified as Arsinoë II cast in
the third century B.C. or to another of the Ptolemaic Arsinoës which is
in Boston, but is a mediocre marble.[25] Carpenter's attempt also to link
the Boy from Tralles to a new period is novel but unconvincing on the
basis of his estimate of it, "leaning cloaked against a blank stone
pier, empty of action yet so sophisticatedly full of charm."[26] More
acceptable is the date early in the first century B.C. assigned to it
by the book he was reviewing,[27] which appears, in the absence of
evidence to the contrary, to be true of several of these problematic
pieces Carpenter has collected as examples "even though the extreme
restraints with which the advanced third century delights in naturalistic veridicity has misled more than one student into undervaluing its
accomplishments," and the writer may be the one who is misled.

While there was indeed a naturalistic phase to this period of Greek
sculpture, it was balanced by the more energetic treatment to an
increasing degree of most figure sculpture, climaxed by the first
Attalid dedication. In this famous group of heroic dead and dying can
be seen a pivotal movement, whose balance between inward and expansive
compositional devices makes it both the embodiment or summation of the
first period and a forecast of the progressive dynamism of the second
Hellenistic epoch. In the schemes of Carpenter, Krahmer, and Bieber,
it occupies the same significant position, regardless of whether the

chronological division between the first and second periods is placed at the beginning or end of the third quarter of the third century before our era.[28] The theme and the scale and manner in which it is carried out are a prelude to what is to come. Like the earlier part of the first period of Hellenistic art, the second is also introduced by a technical phase about several decades in duration, at whose conclusion we may place the well-known marble sleeping satyr restored by Bernini, in Munich, and the equally fine bronze sleeping Eros belonging to the Metropolitan Museum in New York, both variously dated around the turn of the century.[29] They indicate conclusively the presence in this period of artists magnificently qualified in the technical and formal sense, and summarize effectively the tradition of naturalism of the latter half of the third century B.C.

In the meantime, a group of Gauls and Persians, smaller in scale, but possibly greater in number than the earlier collection, had been cast in bronze to be dedicated on the Acropolis in Athens by Attalus I, probably in 201 B.C. At least their resemblance to the first dedication, and the similarity between the sleep of death of the later group and the sleeping satyr and Eros makes this date most likely, for they would indeed be peculiar contemporaries with the later Hellenistic work of the mid-second century B.C.[30] Whatever set in motion the most ambitious architectural and sculptural project in all Greek art -- the altar and two friezes at the capital of the Pergamene kingdom -- is unknown, but undoubtedly the visit to Athens by Attalus I played an important part.

In 197 B.C. his son and successor Eumenes II, the first ruler to have
his own image stamped on Pergamene coins subsequent to that of the
founder Philetairos, ascended the throne. The riches of Pergamon
included a library, complete with scholars and "pergama" or parchment,
in emulation of the Ptolemaic capital, but apparently it was felt to
lack a comparable religious center, like the Serapeum, to show the
Hellenistic world who the true standardbearers of the Greek tradition
were. At any rate there is nothing more mysterious about the inspiration behind the altar, whose form was one of long standing, than there
was about the Periclean program in Athens.[31] The result at Pergamon was
a monument truly comparable to the Parthenon, or to Hagia Sophia, its
veritable successor in importance, yet it has been regarded as less
successful than either. The reasons are not difficult to ferret out,
and they reveal the significance of the great frieze to later Hellenistic art.

Most importantly, its character, in spite of its pomposity and
bombast, is essentially that of an idealistic revival. Like all such,
its overwhelming desire to express again the artifices of another age
led to a dead end, for artistic originality became subordinate to the
attempt to infuse passion into artistic formulas not designed for the
task. The second flaw lay in the very consistency of its unremitting
multiple diffusion of divine force, as the entire Greek Pantheon
battles its adversaries at fever pitch. A third is the absence of a
sufficient number of features presented in human terms or scale, so that

it is less knowable to the mind, although it may be doubted that the Athena Parthenos, which the Attalids had reproduced, was any more humanistic when seen in its original scale.

The erection of the altar was not only an impressive tour de force of the first magnitude, worthy of our respect and admiration, for later Greek art it surpassed the point of no return. Several factors conspired to make this sure. It is due to the perspicacious study of Carpenter that we owe our awareness of the shift during the sculpture of the middle Hellenistic period from a glyptic to a plastic approach, from an emphasis upon carving to one featuring modelling.[32] At the same time, a new angularity, linearization and hardness of construction have been interpreted correctly as the first steps in a progressive neo-atticism which were to culminate in Augustan classicism, as the bodily plasticity of all Greek art began here to be replaced by the appearance of volume.[33] To these two observations should be added another, for to the writer it seems that the difference between the backgrounds of the gigantomachy and Telephus friezes is equally important. On the first, the gods and giants project in very high relief, carrying to its farthest possible extent the increasing density and unyielding quality which was seen beginning with the developing atrophy of relief sculpture in the late fourth century B.C. Attic grave reliefs. There are few reliefs during the third century but statues were apparently often intended to be placed against a wall, like the _fanciulla_ of Anzio, self-sufficient, and isolated against a background.[34] In the Telephus frieze, conventionally dated around 164-158 B.C., a new style of continuous narrative, with the scenes separated by landscape devices, is initiated, whose significance for the pictorial characteristics of Roman painting and relief should be emphasized. It is clearly important for the final phase of Greek art, because it is completely in accord with the rise of a plastic point of view and the incipient classicism of Pergamene art of the second quarter of the second century B.C.[35] The artists of Pergamon, drawn from the entire Hellenistic koiné, were the first to regard the background of a relief as something more than a forbidding barrier, before which figures must be displayed. To the classic Greek world, which regarded space as neutral, there succeeded, as the byproduct of the spatial experimentation of the third century in statuary, a crystallized understanding of its positive implications for relief. Without the Greek discovery of the potentialities of the background plane, the so-called Hellenistic pictorial reliefs would not have been possible. With it, the late Hellenistic period, whose total duration may be carried down to the Augustan revival of the fifth century style, begins.

The final age of Hellenistic art is so different in character from the third century B.C., a logical continuation of later classic, that it is difficult to appraise the many trends within it. Still it is divisible into fairly clearly marked phases which, like the preceding periods, appear to have endured between twenty and thirty years in length, although Hellenistic chronology is by no means as precise as the railroad timetable it has sometimes been made to seem.[36] The first

direction continued the new possibilities opened up by the two friezes
and their companion works such as the Nike of Samothrace, with its
carefully arranged setting, as foremost consideration was given to the
further exploration of every known theme and manner to the limit, as the
Aphrodite of Syracuse.[37]  In place of the primary emphasis of prior
periods upon naturalism or poses or techniques, this phase appeared to
feature novelty for its own sake to enliven types long familiar.  Its
uneven multiplicity of style has as a common denominator the steady
reduction of three-dimensional massivity in favor of its concentration
into a frontal view.  The "einansichtige" groups of mythological figures
are one-sided due to their makers' new awareness of depth as an illusionistic device.  Other indications that it was not caused by a sudden
inability to render plasticity, but a change in direction of interest
resulting in an apparent loss of three-dimensionality, are the afore-
mentioned Hellenistic reliefs and the increased transfer of motifs
between painting and the realm of sculpture.[38]  These developments,
however, did not reach their height until the end of the second century
B.C. and after, but were active as artistic undercurrents, like the
steady development of archaism into Roman neo-atticism.

In the meantime a kind of formal consolidation based upon Attic
prototypes offered an escape when these variegated currents swept
dangerously close upon the verge of artistry, and Hellenistic art
refounded itself on the solider base of classic tradition, primarily at
the commercial centers of Rhodes and Delos.  Their business taste

embraced such works as the Aphrodite of Melos (Pls. LII), and the motley

inhabitants, eager for respectability, immortalized themselves by placing

their portraits on classic bodies of mediocre workmanship, carefully

mounted in discreetly conspicuous niches.[39]  The Greeks were becoming

the artists of the entire Mediterranean world, but not all their

pastiches were as feeble as the recreations in Rhodes and Egypt of the

crouching Aphrodite (Pls. XII, XXII), for the third-century Doidalsas

was now an old master too, and the smoothly competent surface undu-

lations of the well-known Aphrodite found at Cyrene (Pls. XLIII, XLIV)

show what heights of skill were attainable.  At a more prosaic level the

post-Praxitelean *sfumato* became no more than a mere manner of modelling.

The final revivification of Greek sculpture came with the surpri-

singly discriminating patronage of Rome itself, in the last century

before Christ, although it may be begging the question to call the

brutal bronze boxer by Apollonios Nestoros Greek rather than Roman.  The

Laokoon and the type of the blind Homer, but not the so-called Helle-

nistic ruler, reveal an oddly powerful and rhetorical combination of

Roman republican verism, neo-classicism, and the heritage of Pergamon.[40]

These traits, more sharply accentuated through an angular linearization,

appear after all on the renowned green basalt bust of Julius Caesar in

Berlin, the last significant portrait of the Roman republican period.

The most decisive accomplishment within the Hellenistic plastic tra-

dition, portraiture, was to permeate Roman and all later Western art.

### 3. Changing Concepts of Aphrodite

The goddess of love and fertility retained some of the powers among the Greeks that had been hers in the Near East. Pausanias (1.14.7) reports that the rites of Aphrodite _Urania_ had been introduced into Athens by King Porphyrion, meaning that her cult came in with Phoenician commerce.[41] By extensions of her connection with trade, she was associated with seafaring as Aphrodite _Euploia_, or appeared armed as the protectress of a city as at Corinth. The epithet _Urania_, the Semitic Queen of Heaven, or the Greek _Pandemos_, goddess of the whole people, were evidences of her symbolic control over mundane and cosmic generative activities in both the human and natural spheres, whose worship ensured good fortune in many affairs of life. As one of the twelve major deities, in the Hellenic pantheon, by the fifth century B.C. she had acquired the ultimate accolade of being represented a number of times by Pheidias, to whom may be traced a standing figure of her with one foot on a tortoise, in the collection in Berlin.[42] But the upheaval in Greek culture attendant upon the Peloponnesian wars made that type of image in which the impression of divine majesty shone uppermost less satisfying. The humanization of divinity, visible in the sculpture traceable to the fourth century B.C., initiated several centuries of freedom with respect to the creation of new types, in which the humanity of a beautiful mortal, though godlike, became ever more and more prominent.[43] It is of particular importance for the study of statues of Aphrodite that the more active centers of Hellenistic civilization really lay to the East of Greece proper, and that artists were brought closer to the areas from which the goddess had come long

ago.  In retrospect, it seems almost inevitable that the sculptors of

the Ionian coastal region should have played the leading role they did

in the creation of Aphrodite types during the third and second centuries

B.C.  In contact, through both trade and war, with the Near East, their

work was nevertheless solidly based on Greek precedent, upon whose

tradition they built until the culmination of Pergamene art, itself of

Attic inspiration, early in the second century B.C.  It will be seen

that this implies there was a steady continuation into the third

century before Christ of certain distinctive traits initiated during the

fourth, as was pointed out above in the discussion of the evolution of

Hellenistic sculpture.

The representation of Aphrodite followed realignments in culture

and religion closely.  The closer one looks at later Greek civilization,

the more evident it becomes that the period of Alexander the Great,

however disruptive it may have been politically, was a time when the

Greeks clung all the more tenaciously to their standards, in the face of

the political transformations which were taking place.  There were

changes but, for the sculpture of Aphrodite, the really fundamental

shifts occurred after the Athenian downfall of 400 B.C. and the Perga-

mene ascendancy of about 200 B.C.  One may support such an interpre-

tation by reference to the conclusions of an historian of ancient

religion.  M. P. Nilsson has concluded that the first great crisis of

Greek faith in this era, coinciding with the defeat of Athens, amounted

to a breaking up of the old religious sentiment.[44]  The third century
was a continuation of the fourth with wider horizons, in which cult
worship included kings as well as gods, and with philosophy more and
more replacing religion.  The reduction of cult worship and religion to
superstition on a popular level brought on the next crisis, which Nilsson
placed around 200 B.C. and characterized as a conversion to credulity in
religious affairs.  The material, intellectual, and political foundations of life in the Hellenistic states were deprived of any possibility
of future growth, and threatened, if not overrun, by the Roman legions.
In art, however, the weakened creative originality of the old tradition
was balanced by experiments in the second and first centuries B.C.
essential to the success of the arts under Rome.  Viewed in terms of the
representations of Aphrodite, a Hellenistic sequence should commence in
the fourth century B.C. with the statue from Arles in the Louvre,
associated with Praxiteles (Pl. I,b).[45]  It can be better studied from
the cast in Arles, made before its restoration by Girardon (Pl. I,a),
and should be dated around 350 B.C.  The first famous half-nude figure
of the goddess, its drapery extends across the lower stomach in a large
roll, is caught up by the left arm, and falls in sweeping folds to the
feet.  The largeness of modelling is matched by the broad planes of the
bared, longwaisted torso, and the gentle effect is enhanced by a
modestly bowed head.  The whole impression in the original must have
been one of serene, somewhat impersonal grace, nicely expressing the
fifth-century majesty of a divine presence.

Shortly afterward in time may be placed the Aphrodite of Capua, on
account of its similar proportions and drapery, which has been linked to
the name of Scopas.[46] In contrast to the frontality of the Arles figure,
here the most meaningful view is from the side, and opposed to the
reflective dreaminess of the former the latter, to be restored writing
on a shield, was engaged in a specific activity. The bronze original,
made for the temple at Acrocorinth, mentioned by Pausanias (2.5.1),
seems to have been the first well known half-nude cult image of
Aphrodite.

Beyond question one of the most renowned depictions of the goddess
in ancient sculpture was the Aphrodite of Praxiteles at Cnidos, referred
to by Athenaeus (Deipnosophistae 13.59), Clement of Alexandria (Protrept.
53), Lucian (Images 6, Amores 13) and Pliny (N.H. 36.20-22) among others,
shown here in a late Hellenistic bronze replica now in the Metropolitan
Museum in New York (Pl. II).[47] It does not, like the others cited here,
need another descriptive account added to those which have been made of
it from antiquity onwards to the modern age, for its apt combination of
subject matter, naturalism, soft modelling, and instinctive gesture
succeeded in making it one of the most influential pieces for the
history of Hellenistic and indeed of Western art. The features relevant
to later Aphrodite representations do, however, require comment. It
seems to be the last monumental classic creation in which one can detect
an emphasis upon frontality, but simultaneously there is a new three-
dimensional quality, for a three-quarter view and one of the fully

modelled back are almost equally meaningful. More important, as the
goddess disrobes herself, she looks outward, conscious of herself in
time and space, a distinct personality with a sense of existence in a
slightly embarrassing condition, as indicated by her pose. Head turned
to her left, the right hand is placed across her bust, and her left,
about to lay her garment on a hydria, has paused in front of her hips;
it is the forerunner of the pudica attitude. The result is a new sense
of isolation, withdrawal, and consolidation, of separateness from the
surroundings in which she nevertheless existed, in a special shrine at
Cnidos, apart from the everyday world. For Aphrodite as a goddess, this
was a shift from the timeless to the timely; as a work of sculpture it
established a new spatial relationship; as a depiction of the human
figure it set future artists on the road to ever more naturalistic and
personal representation of the deity. Its date lay within the third
quarter of the fourth century B.C.

Following the innovations of Praxiteles in marble there seem to
have been created a few small bronzes of the nude Aphrodite with an
uncertain gesture. A representative example is in the British Museum
(Pls. XI, XII), datable to c. 300 b.c.; another is in New York (Pl.
VIII); a later version is in Providence (Pls. VI, VII).[48] In these
something of the grace and fullness of Praxitelean modelling may be
recovered, as well as the survival of a frontal emphasis, heightened by
the upraised arms and hands which may have been adjusting a necklace,
or, in another type, putting on the sword of Ares.[49] One might note

that a similar gesture, in which both hands were raised to wring water from the hair, appeared in the famous painting of Aphrodite _Anadyomene_ by Apelles at Cos at about this time (Pliny, _N.H._ 35.79,91). In sculpture, the identical motive was not used until a later date.

The final influential work in the above category of female statues made near the beginning of the Hellenistic epoch is the Medici Aphrodite (Pl. III), so called from the type statue in the Uffizi in Florence of an original made around the turn of the century.[50] Praxiteles, his sons, or even Lysippus have been suggested as the artist, although there is not enough evidence to decide. It is most profitable to contrast the Medici marble replica of a bronze original of Aphrodite with the Cnidian, for it continues the softened rendering of Praxiteles and other fourth-century artists to create flesh, hair, and a face instantly comprehensible as feminine. Yet alongside of this somewhat exaggerated, indistinct  _sfumato_ appears a new and specific precision in the pudica gesture, so that the female attributes, though concealed, are emphasized in an almost coquettish manner. There is a mincing stylishness to the attitude, forecasting the artificiality or deliberate pomposity of later Hellenistic style, while the quarter spiral of the position, feet front, head to the side, sets a pattern for many of the standing figures made during the third century B.C.

All traces of frontality had disappeared by the middle decade of the third century, with the creation of the crouching Aphrodite type, whose pyramidal form invited admiration from all sides (Pls. IX, X,

XIII).[51] Of greater importance here is the effect upon her character as
interpreted by future artists, for the concept amounts in fact to a
genre figure and a much more remote link with the Olympian realm of
divinity. Although the motive was derived from the earlier depiction of
a bride in her ritual bath, there is no question but that it was a
formal and psychological monument of the first magnitude. As such, it
will be discussed in detail in the next chapter.

The following Aphrodite type is a veritable missing link in
Hellenistic sculpture. It is the Aphrodite Anadyomene as a plastic
image, taken over, like the croucher, from two-dimensional art, which
itself is proof that this practice began before the second century
B.C.[52] A half-draped example exists in the Vatican (Pl. XL), with a
head from another statue of the same type.[53] The smoothly parted hair,
with its locks close to the head, is in the style of the third century
B.C., similar to the coiffure of Arsinoë III, who reigned from 222 to
209 B.C. (Pl. XX). The heavy-handed treatment of the drapery is due to
its restoration, but in the body may be perceived the exceptional
naturalism, seen especially in the rounded forms and the triangular
navel, echoing the kind of modelling then in vogue. It may have been
nearly contemporary with the nude version, if Carpenter, in positing the
third quarter of the third century as a phase of unexaggerated naturalism, is correct in placing in it the original of the Aphrodite of
Cyrene.[54] On the basis of stylistic and other evidence, the type fits
this period better than any other, for its naturalistic but tight

carving of the female form makes it an apt parallel to the crouching type, and its full nudity invites appreciation from all sides. The pose also implies an almost complete psychological preoccupation within oneself and a lack of self-consciousness characteristic of Hellenistic sculpture during the middle of the third century and lasting till its end.[55]

A presentation of Aphrodite marked by its sincerity as a formal study, yet forecasting to some degree the artfulness of the late Hellenistic period, is the type known as the sandalbinder, which can be dated to the end of the third century before Christ (Pls. XIV-XVIII, XXI-XXVI), as is shown in Chapter Three of this investigation. The genre motif has here succeeded in making the goddess little more than a mortal woman. Balancing on one foot, her pose will soon change, and the sense of space and time initiated by Praxiteles a century or more earlier has here been brought to its full fruition.

The moment had come for a reappraisal, for the character of the goddess was not suited to the kind of heroic activity seen on the large frieze at Pergamon, although she was portrayed there.[56] A change of direction occurred, which, however, took place in terms of past tradition, and hence none of the creations of Aphrodite after 200 B.C. possess quite the same kind of originality. Since the late Hellenistic period eventually revised and reproduced almost every known type of the deity, one can only indicate the more significant examples here. The first to be noted is the Capitoline image, recently dated persuasively

between 200 and 150 B.C. (Pl. XXXVI).[57]  It is a direct recasting of the
Medici version, a parallel to the reworking of the Athena Parthenos at
Pergamon.[58]  Her amplitude of form, the protective gesture of her hands
placed almost against the body, and her stylish coiffure recall the old
bearing and manner, but with a difference, for she is here another
being, a magnificent figure, but no longer a goddess.  Her generative
powers were now to be interpreted as a capacity to charm, to delight.
The semi-divine majesty has gone too in the numerous variations on a
theme of falling drapery (Pls. XXXVII, XXXVIII), or the well-known
Syracuse example.[59]  These were common from the mid-second century on,
and this phase of experimentation extended to nude types also, yet one's
pleasure in viewing these classicistic pastiches with their exceptionally soft modelling is limited largely to an interest in their technical
ingenuity.  They are pleasant, but perfectly human presentations of the
goddess.

Around 100 B.C. were made three works illustrating varied conceptions of Aphrodite near the end of the Hellenistic era.  The Delos
group, now in Athens, of Aphrodite, Pan, and Eros, in which the goat
god's erotic advances are being warded off by a slipper, preserves the
old pudica gesture.[60]  Technically undistinguished, it reveals apparently the final collapse of the harmonious balance between spiritual
strength and physical appeal of the Aphrodite tradition.  Yet two other
figures prove decisively that images of the divinity with the power to
inspire could still be made.  One is the half-clad Aphrodite of Melos,

a highly successful rephrasing of the tradition of the fourth century
B.C. (Pl. LII).[61] The other is the nude Cyrene figure, in which one can
see once more that blend of idealism and naturalism which it was the
Greek genius to convey (Pls. XLIII, XLIV).[62] The longwaisted proportions, which had not been used since 350 B.C., return, and the
symbolic force of a goddess in human form is recaptured through a
deliberate and dexterous classicism.

## CHAPTER II

THE CROUCHING APHRODITE TYPE AS AN ILLUSTRATION OF THE

CHARACTER OF EARLY HELLENISTIC SCULPTURE


Scattered among the museums of the Old and the New World, as well as in private collections, there exists a type of ancient statue of the Greek goddess Aphrodite long recognized as reproducing a famous original.[1] The nude goddess is shown crouching, apparently in conjunction with bathing. Such an association was first made acceptable by the renowned creation of Aphrodite by Praxiteles, set up in a specially constructed shrine at Cnidus in Asia Minor about 350 B.C. As opposed to the standing pose of the Attic master Praxiteles, the crouching version emphasizes a heaviness of hip and thigh which makes for an impression more feminine and less divine than the mid-fourth century statue. The origin of the crouching Aphrodite type has been tangibly solved, but its significance in the development of later Greek art remains insufficiently noted. Before proceeding to an analysis of its importance, it is desirable to fix the identity of the type by describing it in some detail, and by reviewing both ancient evidence and modern interpretations.

1.  Description and Replicas of the Type

Perhaps the finest surviving marble example was discovered at the villa in Tivoli of the Roman Emperor and art collector Hadrian in the early 1920's, and now graces the Museo delle Terme in Rome (Pls. IX, X).[2] Life size, its measurements correspond within a centimeter to two copies in the Louvre, one from Vienne (Pl. XIII), the other from Tyre.[3] The first mentioned, however, is the only one of the three to preserve a part of the head in the original attitude. Crouching down, the nude Aphrodite supports herself by sitting on the heel of her right foot, which, because her knee is bent straight forward, is directly beneath her right side. The left leg is in a squatting position, and its knee is also projected forward, but sharply up. The line of Aphrodite's lower left leg slopes back under her, and both heel and toes of her left foot rest on the ground. The support thus furnished is far from static, and the general impression is of a figure carefully balanced and full of life. For, in order to maintain her equilibrium, the goddess leans forward slightly so that her weight falls on both legs.

To learn how the arms and head were arranged in the original, one may examine not only the Terme marble, but also a complete and unrestored bronze statuette in Copenhagen, and a restored full size marble in the Vatican from a Roman bath on the Via Praenestina (Pl. X).[4] The left arm drops down and across the lower part of her body, the forearm resting on her left thigh. The right arm of the goddess bends down from her shoulder, which is stretched somewhat forward so that her elbow is roughly in front of the middle of her body. Her right forearm is

extended up over the left shoulder, with the fingers curled as if she
were about to adjust her hair at the back of her neck. The upper hand
of the Vatican piece has been restored. Her head is tilted forward and
turned sharply to her right, making her gaze follow a line out over the
left shoulder and downwards at the same time. Her hair is arranged in
short, gently waving locks particularly prominent over the temples with
a bow of hair at the crown, and down the back of her head is a combination of small locks and short tresses. In general, the form of the body
is large and rather massive, a characteristic which is emphasized by
folds of flesh across the stomach, accentuated, as are the ample hips,
by the attitude itself.

Lists of the extant examples have been published by Bernoulli,
Klein, Kaschnitz-Weinberg, and Lullies.[5] There are some two dozen
statues, of which a goodly proportion are life size, as well as a number
of statuettes, and several terra cottas. Klein's list was divided into
three groups. He took as his type figure, his group "a," the excellent
statue from Vienne mentioned above (Pl. XII). His group "b" accounted
for those figures in which the right knee sinks to or toward the ground.
Klein's group "c" is identical to his "b" so far as the right leg is
concerned, but in "c" the right arm is raised higher and is placed more
to the rear, making the figure more erect. He also attempted to establish a chronological sequence, labeling his groups the ancient counter-
parts of baroque, rococo, and style empire. Kaschnitz-Weinberg pretty
well demolished Klein's categories, pointing out that the differences
are largely due to the work of restorers. Evidence does speak for an

opening out of the composition in subsequent modifications of the original conception.  First, however, there is more to be said in relation to the creation of the type.

## 2.  Attribution of the Crouching Aphrodite

The origin of the figure has been related to a passage in the elder Pliny's Natural History (36.36), where the extant manuscripts exhibit a considerable divergence in the text.  In the course of listing statues collected in Rome, one of them is described as Venerem lavantem se sedaedalsas stantem Polycharmus in the Bamberg manuscript, but the Riccardianus and Vossianus read sesededalsa.[6]  Theodore Reinach would replace the ae or e in the first syllable of daedalsas by the dipthong oe to recover the name Doedalsas or the Dorian Δοιδαλσας which, he points out, was a name associated by Strabo with Asia Minor.[7]  It also occurs in Memnon, an historian of Heraclea Pontica in the first century A.D., an inscription from Nicomedia, another from Kermasli, and in the writings of Eustathios, whose particular text at this point, Reinach states, is a fragment of Arrian's History of Bithynia, describing a sculptor named Daidalos, whose masterpiece was a statue of Zeus Stratios at Nicomedia.  Equating this Daidalos with the Daedalsas of Pliny, now corrected as Doidalsas, Reinach emerges with the name of a Greek sculptor, Doidalsas of Bithynia.  Since the founding of Nicomedia dated from 264 B.C., and a statue presumed to be the Zeus Stratios appears on coins of Nicomedia starting with the reign of Prusias I, from about 218 B.C. on, we are given two dates to assist in placing the crouching Aphrodite within the development of Hellenistic sculpture.

The above sketch of Reinach's bold identification omits one other important point. While he may have settled, as well as it can be done, the question of the obscure passage in Pliny and the identification of the sculptor of the <u>Venerem lavantem se</u> as Doidalsas of Bithynia, the text only refers to a bathing Aphrodite. How then is it related to the prototype of the various copies of the crouching figure? First suggested, according to Reinach, by Guattani in his <u>Monumenti Inediti</u> in 1788, the supposition has been renewed by other scholars, including Bernoulli in 1873, but was opposed by Sellers in 1896, affirmed by Reinach a year later, and supported by Klein the year following.[8] Since the turn of the century it seems generally to have been accepted.

The identification has been strengthened by the existence of a group of coins from Asia Minor of Imperial date, presenting on their obverses an image of the statue. Bernoulli, Klein and Bernhart give lists, which support an attribution of the type to the area, proving the coins were centered about Bithynia.[9] From West to East, the principal issues run as follows: one is a bronze of Julia Domna from the island of Chios off the coast; one was issued under Severus Alexander from Nicaea in Bithynia proper; and another from Claudiopolis in Honorias, included in Eastern Bithynia from about the second century A.D. on. Farther to the East, the fourth and fifth were struck under Septimius Severus, one showing the emperor on its obverse, the other, his wife Julia Domna. Both come from Gangra-Germanicopolis in Paphlagonia, which was a part of the province of imperial Bithynia. The last is from the city of Amisus in Pontus, East of Bithynia, and bears the earliest date, 137/8 A.D.

The figure shown on the coins matches the statue type beyond reasonable doubt. The same strong turn of the head to the right, and the raised left knee, are preserved in both. The addition of one or more Erotes, each holding a torch or mirror, may reflect the incorporation of the crouching Aphrodite in a group. Whether or not the statue was conceived as a single figure is not revealed by the copies, for there are replicas with and without traces of an Eros, but any estimate should also be influenced by one's idea of the material of the original work, as well as of its character.

### 3. Conception of the Original

The presence of an Eros and of artificial supports below the left side in the example from Vienne were necessary in that marble version for stability (Pl. XIII, cf Pl. XXIV center). If the original were of bronze, the Eros would have been structurally superfluous. This is one of the points brought forward by Lippold, who discusses the figure in his _Kopien griechischer Statuen_.[10] To avoid running into difficulty with Pliny, who lists the _Venerem lavantem se_ as a statue in marble, he supposes that the one familiar to Pliny was itself a copy, and that a bronze original existed in Asia Minor. Those copies found in the East, he states, adhere most closely to the coin image. S. Reinach, in his publication of the small bronze from the Durighello collection in the Louvre, supports the theory of a bronze original, stating that the ancients "never" copied a marble original in bronze.[11] For considering the crouching figure as a bronze, however, the example in Copenhagen lacks the peculiarities of gesture and attitude which render the

Durighello bronze, whose formal characteristics are distinctly different from other versions, almost suspect. A comparison of the position of the hands and of the overall proportions reveals a sinuous grace which is definitely not in keeping with the Ny Carlsberg example (Pl. X). Concerning the original choice of material, no one seems to have noticed how much more reasonable the fleshy folds on the stomach appear when visualized in bronze, or that the hair style is really designed for that kind of precise treatment of individual locks best rendered in bronze, and which the marble copyists seem clearly to have been attempting within the limits of their own material. It seems most reasonable, therefore, to conclude that the first creation was in bronze, from these considerations alone.

In looking at the execution of the example from Tivoli, now in the Museo delle Terme, one is struck by the quality of the face (Pls. IX, X). Its expression is quiet and restrained, and has behind it the best tradition of generalization, if not of idealization, inherent in Greek sculpture. The features convey an impression which conflicts sharply with the very specific effect given by the representation of the torso. In order to produce the heavy rounded folds banding the abdomen, the stone has been cut into deep, shadow catching grooves. After noticing the comparative restraint in the carving of the head, the jarring effect caused by the necessarily different manner of surface representation of the anatomy is yet another point in favor of an original in bronze, whose overall emphasis would have been more uniform, in short, more like the Copenhagen bronze statuette (Pl. X).

The character of the original may be best perceived by examining the two replicas just cited, which, because of their comparative clarity of conception, may well echo the bronze original closely. As opposed to the example once in the Cook collection, for instance (Pl. XXIV, center), the Terme piece (Pl. IX) preserves a somewhat simpler outline. Its volume forms an entity in itself. The adjustment of the figure within a rather egg-shaped envelope, whose heavier end is at the bottom, illustrates the technical facility of the artist and his ability to articulate volume (cf. Pl. XIII). The horizontal right leg provides a visual balance for the rest of the body in front of the left leg, whose upward pointing knee starts the observer's eye off around the statue. The complex shifting of solids and voids in and around the arms fills the area between the knees and the head without creating a gap in the contour. The turn and thrust of the head create a new emphasis in a different direction but, like the arms, do not break through the overall outline. Running down the other side, the volume's limits are now controlled by, as well as being identical to, the solid, unbroken expanse of the back and the predominant interest becomes the surface modelling rather than the relation to space. When one's gaze reaches the base, one finds that a complicated system of weight and support is dealt with clearly. The ankle bridges the gap between the tectonic support of the right foot, and the visual one of the right thigh and leg with their joint horizontal line. Notice that this brief glance at the statue is made from one point of view. One finds the richest variety equated with the greatest sense of a statue in three dimensions when studying the work from this angle. Walking around the crouching figure, this balance is lost (Pl. X). From the front, the position of the arms complicates matters. When seen from the left side, the left leg predominates, giving a slimmer and more vertical effect until the head appears, swinging sharply to the right (Pl. IX). The back is a fine study in modelling where one sees only the outer shell of the form whose interior is so richly filled from a more frontal vantage point.

The foregoing stylistic analysis has focussed attention upon a work whose original material is presumed to have been bronze. The discussion remains incomplete, however, until the question of whether or not the crouching figure was paired with an Eros is dealt with. From a practical point of view, the addition of an Eros would have contributed to the stability of the crouching Aphrodite. As a group, the two-figure composition, it might be argued, would be linked to those groups which distinguished the sculpture of the second half of the third century B.C. These, however, are different in subject for they are either fighting Greeks or Gauls. Both are conceived as being slightly larger than life size, and the crouching figure, just over a meter in height, is about one-quarter more than full scale. Such a comparison does not really, however, increase the likelihood that the goddess was thought of originally as forming part of a group. Similarly, to argue that Aphrodite needed a complementary mythological personage to establish a motive, an Eros pouring bathwater or holding a mirror seems to rely overmuch upon wishful comparisons with such erotic groups as the Delos "pantoufle" example or place too heavy an emphasis upon the imperial coins, which

do not agree among themselves.[12] Also, Pliny says nothing about any
other figure. One must consider this question upon the primary evidence
of the statue itself. The single figure is neither a distinct nor
erotic subject, and its formal characteristics would be altered were it
not a single unit. Any addition would destroy the well-thought-out
three dimensionality of the kneeling goddess; by extending the composition sideways it would become flatter and suffer a loss of its
monumental simplicity. On the other hand, the presence of an Eros in
later times, added by subsequent artists, is perfectly reasonable.

### 4. Historical Significance of the Type

Enough has been said to make clear a number of conceptual differences in contrast to the classical age as seen in earlier works, which
the crouching Aphrodite, a monumental and original creation of the mid-
third century B.C. nevertheless exemplifies. More than most works of
that period, it demonstrates both the similarities which tie it to the
older tradition and the differences which distinguish it as something
new and set forth clearly some of the changes in the sculpture of the
early Hellenistic epoch. Any great creative work can be looked at for
its possession of these two aspects. To see how this figure contains
within itself not only the fruits of tradition but also the seeds of
innovation, it should be compared and contrasted with other outstanding
works of Greek sculpture from the period between c. 350 and c. 250
before Christ.

First, the image of the crouching Aphrodite preserves that sense of harmonious unity associated with works dating from earlier times. There is about the statue an effect of life which owes its existence to the vigor and balance with which many of the elements basically inherent in sculpture are employed. One notes the ponderation, or system of weight and support with respect to the ground, the careful construction of volume and the harmonious attention to surface contributing to a balanced emphasis upon the finished product as a whole. The complex though quiet air of this statue in terms of volume and space, a kind of completeness within itself, helps to produce a psychological mood of restraint, differing somewhat from productions of an earlier date. Contrasted with the first famous statue of Aphrodite in a state of undress the masterpiece by Praxiteles at Cnidos, it is evident that the latter can not quite overcome a certain almost surreptitious relation to the spectator.[13] Aphrodite stands in her shrine, as if she were in her own bath, but the entrance has not been barred, and it is as if one had penetrated to view the goddess of beauty in a private act. There is here a definite self-consciousness and lack of ease. The same is true, of course, for the Medici type, whose original creation is also datable to the late fourth century B.C. (Pl. III).[14] This equally famous presentation of the goddess is also a self-conscious one, but the emphasis is all the other way. The spectator's eye is drawn to the female attributes, and there is here a frank invitation to admire. Both types lean well forward, and even though they are placed firmly on both feet in standing positions, their poses help to contribute to the uneasy aspect.

Formally, the crouching Aphrodite should be less stable, considering her position, but she is not. Furthermore, the fact that she has no hydria nor drapery helps to set her apart in her isolation from the spectator.

The tension which develops in Greek art at the end of the fourth century and early in the third, and is present in the stiffness of the Themis from Rhamnus, also has been overcome by the time of Doidalsas' creation.[15] This characteristic is even better exemplified by the austere, angular Demosthenes, whose drapery sets up thrusts and counter-thrusts, upon which is set a head wherein are visible traits of both a classic Greek type and of a realistic portrait.[16] The interest in new poses and effects evident in the Tyche of Antioch, the earliest of such creations of the beginning of the third century B.C., has been absorbed by the time of the crouching Aphrodite and its technique mastered, indicating, even without other evidence, a date at least several decades later.[17] A consequence of this previous period of readjustment is not related to technical aspects of design, but it also affects the mood of the finished product. As a result of the introduction of the female nude for full scale representation of divinity in the fourth century, artists in the third were no longer awed by the idea of divine nudity, and could concentrate more freely on studies of the complete form. For now Aphrodite is oblivious to the absence of garments when confronted with observers, and there is complete concentration upon her activity. No longer are there nervous glances from the face, or instinctive ges-tures of the hands. She is preoccupied at her toilet, and this is the moment chosen, rather than the second after disrobing.

The statue is also significant as a transfer to the field of monumental sculpture of a motif which had long been known. In minor arts, a vase of the Kertsch type and a Corinthian mirror cover, both dating from the fourth century B C., show women or nymphs kneeling in profile.[18] Neither of them can be said specifically to duplicate the pose of the statue discussed here, but, bearing in mind the contemporary depictions of the nude Aphrodite, it is logical to surmise that the crouching goddess is related to such traditions in a less ambitious scale, representing less important figures. Such a conjecture becomes more likely when literary evidence is marshalled to support the theory that the act of bathing has behind it a ritual significance. No less than four different authors tell of the annual festival on the island of Cyprus, where Aphrodite, according to the sixth Homeric hymn, was carried by the sea, and there entered the company of the gods. Athenaeus (s.84c), Strabo (14.683), Ovid (Met. 10.270, and Fasti 4.133) and Aeschines (Epistle 10) report that to commemorate the birth of Aphrodite, the women of Cyprus bathed her image in the sea and then decked it with flowers on the strand of Faphos. Atheneius (13.59091) also describes the festival of Poseidon on the island of Aegina, the Aphrodisia, and tells how Phryne re-enacted the birth of the goddess by putting off her himation, letting down her hair and going into the sea. He continues this anecdote by saying that Apelles made her the model of his painting of Aphrodite Anadyomene. It seems, then, that the creation of a statue in which Aphrodite was depicted bathing, or in an associated personal act, had ample precedent in more than plastic art. From a contemporary point of view, then, the work conformed to Greek religious standards of the day. The more dramatic types of representation, initiated by Praxiteles, echoed in sculpture a parallel emphasis in religious ceremonies. Like the Cnidia, the crouching Aphrodite probably was enshrined alone. One need not regard it as a secular image because it did not conform to the fifth-century Pheidian convention for a cult image, but realize that the croucher was very much a part of a vital classic tradition, modified to suit the taste of the mid-third century B.C.[19]

The differences exhibited by the crouching Aphrodite compared to earlier work are equally significant. The absence of self-consciousness, and the concentration within herself, already noted in contrast to fourth-century images, should be brought out further by comparing the figure with the girl from Anzio. This statue echoes a bronze original created in the middle decades of the third century, and its similarity in spirit to the crouching Aphrodite is so great that it argues for a contemporary date.[20] The Anzio maiden's head is turned to one side and inclined forward so that she looks downward at her tray, whose contents indicate that she is engaged in a religious ritual. The formal complexity is perhaps not as great as that of the crouching figure, but both had crossed their arms in front in order to carry on their respective activities; both have the left foot forward, the right out to one side, and both draped and nude bodies are crisscrossed by diagonals. The correspondence is most notable when comparing the two heads, whose

effects are operative within an area bounded by a tray or a crooked
elbow. Not only is there a great similarity in expression to the extent
of seeming totally detached from the passing world, in the way both
figures look intently down to one side, but also nose, mouth, and cheeks
are modelled with the same soft fullness, even though the girl appears
younger than the goddess. In details, like the wavy locks of hair
around brow and temple, the similarity is very close. Finally, we may
note how both preserve a strong plastic sense, a restraint in modelling,
which gives their presences an air of dignity.

Another aspect of the crouching Aphrodite, shared by the Anzio girl,
is that the statue represents a figure which has been moving, and
clearly will remain only a short time in its present pose, but at the
moment is not in motion. The breakthrough in sculpture to a world of
moving forms, as on the large frieze at Pergamon, followed the creation
of the croucher. Yet, the space around the ovoid envelope of the marble
betrays no evidence of the explosive turmoil which characterizes the
Pergamene relief, and the space within maintains the classical Greek
tradition by helping to preserve a unity of volume and consistent
proportion. There are no sudden variations visible when viewing the
alternations of body and space around the knees and arms which are seen
against the torso.

### 5. Adaptations of the Crouching Aphrodite

Generally speaking, Hellenistic sculpture of the second century
B.C., after the time of the Pergamon altar friezes, more or less ceases

to produce new and original representations, but seems to hark back to extant themes. The unifacial, or frontal aspect, increases, and is accompanied by an indiscriminate adapting and copying of earlier Greek art, so that the result is often a kind of eclecticism. A focus around the face, commented on in the cases of the crouching Aphrodite and the Anzio maiden, no longer holds true in this century which witnessed a loss of direction in sculpture. With this faltering went also a weakening of a clear-cut motivation, until, in some instances, novelty of appearance seemed to be valued more highly than forthright formal statement. Polish and luminosity of finish distinguished many works through the technical brilliance with which these effects were achieved.

In such an atmosphere, a hybrid version of the crouching Aphrodite easily takes its place, and even adds a note of somewhat exotic elegance to the visual setting of the late Hellenistic age. In our own day, there emerged from the bottom of a well on the island of Rhodes a statuette combining the hairbinding gesture of Aphrodite Anadyomene with the kneeling posture of the croucher (Pl. XII, Bottom).[21] Unlike its predecessor studied above, decorative aspects predominate, and the conception is basically two-dimensional. The arms of the figure no longer enfold and limit a centripetal composition; back and head do not bound the volume in unity, and the sagging right leg fails to provide a stable base. The spreading arms, flowing hair, the abruptly cocked left leg -- all conspire to reverse the inner concentration of the original creation of a hundred years earlier. Yet, curiously, the

effect of outward radiation languishes because it starts from no one
well-defined center, but from a broken axis, bisected at the midsection,
so that the upper half, canted and twisted, from sternum to head, sits
askew on a base in a permanent state of imbalance. Thus the inherent
blocklike, pyramidal three-dimensionality of the figure is thwarted, and
the sculptor's search for a novel effect has led to a permanent state of
irresolution, as he subjected his figure to new canons and conceptions
for which it was not designed.

It is amazing how successfully the transformation has been wrought,
and it is small wonder that the result recalls other products of the
period, like a contemporary version of the Aphrodite binding her sandal,
or the renowned image of the goddess from Melos (Pls. XIII, LII).[22]  The
crouching Anadyomene from Rhodes is distinguished from the former
because the sandalbinder's geometry lent itself more easily to second
century standards, and from the latter by its differences of scale and
surface. In place of the academic coolness of the Aphrodite of Melos,
the Rhodian figure charms through the luminosity of its surface. It is
the esthetic appeal of the marble, polished to the point of translucency,
which counteracts the radial character of the composition, and overcomes
the deliberate axial obfuscation with sinuous surface transitions.
Whether today's observer is bemused into sharing in this blurred
delight without protest is beside the point. What is important to
realize is that this little figure served as a vehicle for a technical
tour-de-force, and that the clarity of formal concept of c. 250 B.C.

no longer sufficed in the last half of the second, in the face of the new vistas of pictorial pattern and surface sheen. The fact that the crouching Aphrodite, combined with the _anadyomene_ motif, was capable of surviving these new demands testifies to the significance of the conception.

The _sfumato_ effect so strongly in evidence on the surface of the Rhodian variant seems not to have any relation to Bithynia, but it does recall Alexandrian work, where this sense of translucency was most consistently exploited. When first developed by the followers of Praxiteles, as in the Chios female head in Boston, it was balanced against an equivalent care for structural clarity, which, in Egypt, became subordinated to an excessive softness.[23] Partly because of this same excess of surface attention, the creation of the Rhodian variant has been claimed for Egypt, home of numerous figures of Aphrodite which, on a popular level, often served as wedding presents, being regarded as talismans.[24] The suggestion, on the basis of the similar works published by Adriani, is quite plausible, but can only be tentatively accepted, in view of the widespread popularity of this soft, illusionistic style.

Finally, let us turn back to the form of the bronze original, and consider the one remaining detail not yet discussed, the style of the hair, in connection with the problem of the precise date of the crouching Aphrodite. That coiffure which seems most likely is the one indicated by the statuette in Copenhagen, which has already been selected as one of the type pieces, and which is echoed by the marble

copy in the Terme (Pls. IX, X). A broad ribbon passes over a center
part, and over the crown of the head the hair is combed smooth. Over
the brow, in front of the ribbon, are wavy locks whose different character is overemphasized by the Vatican example, but which for a marble
replica are reliable because the original head sits unbroken on the neck.
The most remarkable feature is a kind of bow, at the very top of the
head, made from long locks drawn up from the back, and joined by the
ends of the tresses starting at the brow. The bow is fastened, not by
a band of ribbon, but by another long lock from the back of the head.
Such an unusual headdress is not without parallels. In the Museum of
Fine Arts, Boston, the Bartlett head illustrates many of the same
details, especially the prominent bow of hair, and the bronze head,
perhaps of Arsinoë II, unfortunately damaged, seems to have had a not
dissimilar topknot.[25] Thus the precedent for this style, set in the
mid-fourth century, carried through the first quarter of the third, for
Arsinoë II died in 270 B.C., to be deified as Aphrodite. The coiffure,
then, favors the earlier decades within the period c. 264-228 B.C., the
outside limits already set for the creation of the crouching Aphrodite.[26]
Finally, we may notice that on the Copenhagen and _Terme_ specimens, a
languidly drooping forelock curls gently in front of the ear (Pls. IX,
X). It resembles the same feature of the head of Arsinoë II, and
differs from the curved "spitcurl" on the temple of Arsinoë III, who
reigned from 222 to 209 B.C. (Pl. XI).[27] The croucher's date should
fall then within a decade of 250 B.C.

It has already been observed that the girl from Anzio and the crouching Aphrodite together exhibit many of the same formal complexities and psychologically introverted traits. These clearly establish the artistic atmosphere of the mid-third century. But it is worthwhile to conclude this chapter with a comparison to another work whose composition is much the same, but whose greater naturalism places it slightly later in time -- the Scythian knife grinder from the Marsyas group.[27] The figure in the Uffizi in Florence may be dated shortly before the first Attalid dedication, c 241-228 B.C. The arrangement of solids and voids in front of the torso corresponds with the crouching Aphrodite in many details. The arms of the Scythian, while not wrapped around the body, enclose the knees, so that a pyramidal volume is manifest from all angles. At the apex of the pyramid the figure turns his head to the left as he looks up to study his prey. The rough hair and naturalistic modelling are close to the treatment of the large Gauls. The greater attention to muscular development compared to the crouching Aphrodite indicates a later stage of the same trend for the Marsyas group, but the near identity of pose, extending even to the same system of weight and support, reveal that these two works were created not more than a dozen-odd years apart.

The sequence thus established from the Anzio maiden and the crouching Aphrodite to the Scythian illustrates the change in the character of sculpture at the close of the early Hellenistic age. The tightly circumscribed forms of the first two are matched by an inwardness of

attitude. Together these aspects set the figures apart from the world
around them, as has been explained above. Such a self-sufficient
quality is the hallmark of the plastic art of the early Hellenistic
period; it is one of the components in the formal characterization and
drapery treatment of the Demosthenes of 280/79 B.C.[28] Beyond the
reasons cited in favor of placing the Scythian later, such as the
greater naturalism, it is the new relationship to his surroundings
displayed by his more studied, but at the same time less artificial and
mannered figure treatment, which distinguishes this creation from its
predecessors. The more open form around the arms and knees, the focus
of attention on something beyond himself, all are new. The grisly
nature of the subject, highlighting a non-Greek in a group composition,
constitutes a foretaste of that combination of naturalism and bellico-
sity, grandeur and passion which became the major themes of the middle
Hellenistic period. But not all the art of c. 250-160 B.C. was dominated by turgid emotionalism. The gentle divinity Aphrodite continued to
appeal, but the outstanding types created in the next epoch exuded an
aura more charming than religious.

CHAPTER III

SPECULATIONS ON THE APHRODITE ANADYOMENE:

HYPOTHESES REGARDING ITS CREATION

The most vexing puzzle in all Hellenistic sculpture is the question
of the origin and development of the Aphrodite Anadyomene, rising from
the sea.[1] It formed the subject of a famous painting by Apelles, active
during the final third of the fourth century, which was at Cos on the
edge of Western Asia Minor until the end of the first century B.C.,
along with another unfinished painting of Aphrodite by the same artist
(Pliny, N.H. 35.92). The city also possessed a statue of the goddess by
Praxiteles, a draped figure, which the inhabitants purchased in preference to the nude image then installed at Cnidos, according to Pliny
(N.H. 36.20). The same industrious compiler described the later fame of
the painting and its fate as follows:[2]

> "His Aphrodite rising from the sea was dedicated by the god
> Augustus in the temple of his father Caesar: she is known as
> the anadyomene, being, like other works of the kind, at once
> eclipsed yet rendered famous by the Greek epigrams written in
> her praise. When the lower portion was damaged no one could be
> found to restore it, and thus the very injury redounded to the
> glory of the artist. In course of time the panel of the picture

fell into decay, and Nero when Emperor substituted for it another picture by the hand of Dorotheos."

The epigrams Pliny referred to, which still survive, have been collected by Overbeck (Schriftcuellen, 1847-1866). The painting showed the upper part of Aphrodite with both hands raised to her hair, from which she was wringing or pressing out the water. The lower portion of the figure was immersed in the sea, through whose transparent waves shone the outline of her body. The picture's renown was great enough so that the sculptor or sculptors who rendered it as a three-dimensional statue in marble or bronze must have been aware of the painting. Thus it is possible to define the motif of the plastic anadyomene as an adaptation, but this does not necessarily detract from the creative originality of the artist who undertook such an assignment. The question is, when, how, and under what circumstance was it done? Up to this point there is general agreement. Beyond that, it is disagreement which is general. A recent, detailed, and objective examination of the earlier conclusions decides, primarily from stylistic analysis, that the half-draped anadyomene was an Aphrodite by Roman times, and that it can be traced to c. 250 B.C. starting perhaps as a genre figure, but that there must have been an interval of at least a century between it and the nude type.[3] Such a time lag seems unnecessarily long, but the earlier date for the partly-clothed image appears to be substantially correct. Let us consider it first.

1. The So-called Half-Draped Anadyomene

The type statue, a marble Roman copy, standing 1.49m., may be seen in the Gabinetto delle Maschere of the Vatican (Pl. XL, cf. Pl. XLI).[4] Parts of the drapery, including the large "Isis" knot, are restored; so is the right arm, and the head comes from another replica of the same type. Aphrodite stands with her weight thrown to her left side so that the other leg is drawn back slightly in a conventional Greek pose with the right heel off the ground (cf. the Medici and the Capitoline figures, Pls. III and XXXVI). Above a torso distinguished by its triangular navel and girlish forms, the hands and arms are raised unevenly to arrange her hair, so the right side is drawn up, and breast, shoulder, and arm are higher on that side, with the hand almost over her head. An opposite slope is established by the drapery, ascending across the hips to the figure's left. The head is bent forward and down rather sharply with a slight turn to her right. It is interesting that the conception differs from the Medici in that Aphrodite is not placed in a deliberate and self-conscious pose, but appears completely relaxed and absorbed in her task, with her arms occupied, so she becomes a study of a figure engaged in the humble act of arranging her tresses, and is only incidentally a goddess. In many ways the conception recalls the maiden from Anzio, whose drapery is also tucked up around her waist to free her hands, while the position of the hands and head reflects the psychological preoccupation it was so clearly the artist's intent to convey.[5] Such an attitude and formal arrangement in the case of the anadyomene

provide a basis for a tentative date in the mid-third century B.C.
One can, however, support it further.

The crouching Aphrodite of about the same time furnishes a number
of distinct parallels. It is another major Hellenistic version in which
the idea of a monumental form is blended with a genre motif to produce
a naturalistic figure study (Pl. X).[6] Yet its pyramidal composition,
topped by a strongly turned head looking outward, perhaps into a mirror
held by Eros, differs enough from the anadyomene type so that one would
seem to have preceded the other, rather than their being contemporary.
One can suspect that they may not be too far apart in time, because
behind both of them there existed a two-dimensional expression of the
same theme in panel or vase painting, although the question of the relationship in general between painting and sculpture in the Hellenistic
period is unsolved.[7]

That evidence which can be advanced in the form of comparative
expressions of similar themes supports a date in the early Hellenistic
period. The motif of upraised arms can be traced easily to several
small post-Praxitelean bronzes of around 300 B.C., like the example in
the British Museum (Pls. XI, XII, cf. Pls. VI-VIII).[8] It can be seen
also in the Praying Boy attributed to Boidas, a bronze with restored
arms in Berlin.[9] On the other hand, the spiralling torsional tendencies
incipient in the Anzio girl, and the pyramidal form of the crouching
Aphrodite, initiate the vigor and characteristic expression of the

heroic groups of the second half of the third century B.C., features which the Aphrodite binding her hair does not share.

One can also accumulate some additional evidence by turning to Egypt. Here the anadyomene type was so well known that Bieber believes it was employed there in an official capacity.[10]

"Next to those of Isis, her (Aphrodite's) attributes were most frequently used in the representation of mortal women. For example, Arsinoë II was venerated as Aphrodite. The main cult statue seems to have been an Aphrodite binding up her hair. As such she appears in many marble statuettes, bronzes and terra cottas, and in molds which were used for bronzes or terra cottas and thus testify to the local fabrication of these statuettes."

There is no question about the widespread popularity of the type, either half or fully nude, in Egypt (Pls. XLVII, XLVIII).[11] The mention of Arsinoë II refers to an edict of her husband Ptolemy II, after her death in 270 B.C., that temples were to be erected in her honor throughout the country, where she was to be worshipped deified as Aphrodite, the first of her line to be so venerated.[12] Presumably the temples would have included a cult statue. It is tempting to think that the image of the half-clad goddess was originated for this purpose, but no evidence supports such an idea.

The costume of the figure in the Vatican was reworked in Roman times, but the head recalls the modelling of face and hair on a head of Arsinoë III in Mantua (Pls. XL, XX).[13] Both heads are in the style of the later third century B.C. It is probable that the "Isis" knot was once less conspicuous, and more in line with other representations of the Isis dress, in which there was a knot between the breasts or at the waist, and a cluster of drapery folds hanging from it down the center of the figure to end at the feet.[14] This feature is unquestionably Egyptian in origin, and examples of knotting the dress about the waist in connection with mourning for the dead are fairly common in the pre-Ptolemaic civilization.[15] In the development of Hellenistic drapery, it has been dated to the second half of the third century B.C.[16] Thus there seems to be every reason to suspect that this Aphrodite figure was Egyptian in origin, and that it first appeared sometime after the middle of the third century before Christ. The writer does not know of a certain full length representation of this queen, but her successors Berenice II, ruler of Cyrene, 258-247 B.C., then queen of Egypt, 247-222 B.C., and Arsinoë III, 222-209 B.C., were both commemorated in statues set up in Egypt, which may be reflected in faience jugs.[17] These show a modest-sized knot and center folds adorning the front of their full-length garments. A small marble statuette of Aphrodite rising from the sea and pressing out her hair from Alexandria itself, later than the third century B.C., now in Copenhagen, seems to illustrate the same knot and folds, although its legs and drapery are incomplete.[18] Often when the anadyonene type, much less common outside Egypt in Hellenistic times, appears elsewhere, it is related to a demonstrable connection with Ptolemaic Egyptian culture. An example has been recovered from the Isis temple in Pompeii.[19] By the Roman era, any distinction between the precise identity of the half-draped and nude versions had long since disappeared. The Pompeiian replica is of the latter variety.

### 2. The Nude Anadyomene

The naked figure has been dated, as stated above, about 150 B.C. by Lullies. His reason was that as an example of late Hellenistic open form it can be no earlier than the mid-second century, which does not seem to be absolutely necessary on those grounds.[20] To maintain that an original of such importance could have been created after the Atticizing work at Pergamon, in a period known for its adaptations of older monuments, is, on the face of it, a shaky assumption. It is also contrary to all the other evidence.

The best example of this type is a classicistic work of great beauty, the marble Aphrodite of Cyrene, whose probable date is approximately 100 B.C. (Pls. XLIII, XLIV).[21] It is a reverse image compared to the half-draped one, and other nude figures of the kind, for the weight is on the right leg, the shoulders slope down to that side, with the arms arranged relatively the same way, but the left, not the right, was higher when the statue was complete. A dolphin at the statue's right supports a cloak whose fringe is similar to the same feature in the case of the Capitoline Aphrodite, dated to the early second century B.C.

(Pl. XXXVI) and its buttonlike navel matches that of the Aphrodites of the Delos group and of Sinuessa (Pl. L, bottom).[22] To appreciate the form of the original, one needs to glance at a mediocre Roman version from the Baths of Caracalla, now in the Museo delle Terme (Pl. L, top).[23] Unfortunately, it too is headless, but the hands holding the tresses give a good idea of its planar organization, almost hieratic in its frontality, typical of the age in which it was carved. Technically, the most impressive example was found near Benghazi, and is now in a private collection, on loan to the University Museum, Philadelphia (Pl. XLVIII).[24] Cut below the hips to sit on a flat surface, which may have been made to imitate water rather than to be joined to drapery-covered legs, it establishes a connection between the painted and plastic images. A bronze from Courtrai (Pl. XLV), reversed like the Cyrene Aphrodite, and a heavily proportioned terra-cotta from the Loeb collection attest to a late Hellenistic popularity (Pl. XLVI). A fine terra-cotta in the Walters Art Gallery is dated to the third century before Christ (Pl. XLVX), and a mould from Egypt proves the popularity of the type there (Pl. XLVII).[25]

Since these statues date, at the earliest, from the second century B.C., and the pieces are headless, placing the original becomes a matter of hypothetical reconstruction of Hellenistic sculpture. Everything known about the second century B.C. indicates that it was not as creative in an original sense as was the third, and to place such a truly great work there would be anachronistic in the extreme.[26] On the other hand, famous older works became sufficiently esteemed to be recreated, like the Capitoline figure.[27] In fact, the Aphrodite of Cyrene is linked to the Capitoline by its fringed garment, as noted above, and at least one author has attempted to date the Cyrene marble itself to the early second century B.C.[28] His link between it and the school of Pergamon is not, however, conclusive, so far as the modelling of the human figure is concerned. Even if the supposition were correct, the disparate treatment of the abdomen and navel of the Cyrene example versus the Capitoline shows that to place the original of the Cyrene figure in that orbit is out of order, for the modelling of the latter lacks the same sense of depth (Pls. XXVI vs. XLIII). There are two standards displayed in the Cyrene Aphrodite. First, one may place the very careful technical finish of the stone's surface to give the impression of skin. Such a treatment is betrayed by the full thighs, svelte stomach, and hard, round navel. In the Capitoline the marble has become skin, genuine flesh, especially in the torso. Second, without prejudice, it may be stated that the Cyrene's construction is neo-classic in that it is so obviously trying to recall something it isn't, through deliberate artifice. To reach the original, one has to pierce through this quality of the torso. Observe the indications of the ribcage beneath the figure's right breast, the indentations at the waist, the bulge of the abdomen, separate from and above the pubic line, the demarcation of the kneecap on both legs. Through the study of these features can be seen the exceptionally acute naturalism which must have been the original's. What other Hellenistic Aphrodite statues can be found with a comparable accuracy of modelling? Certainly it is not to be seen in typical figures of the second century before Christ, like the Aphrodite binding her sandal from the Sabouroff collection (Pl. XXIII).[29] There seems to be no avoiding the fact that the original of the nude anadyomene must precede 200 B.C., the reliefs of the Pergamon altar, and associated work.

Two monuments of the prior period are akin to the type under discussion. The first is the sleeping satyr in Munich.[30] Here one can see the same decisive anatomical modelling on a male figure from about the last decade of the third century, c. 210 B.C. In spite of the plastic affinities in the handling of the stomach, the fact that one arm is raised to the head, and the form exposed fully, the naturalism appropriate to the satyr sleeping off the effects of his revelry does not come as close to the Aphrodite anadyomene, seen through the Cyrene figure, as does another statue type of the same goddess. The crouching image, whose bronze original is dated just prior to 250 B.C., can be studied in several versions, all, like the Cyrene marble, copies (Pls. IX, X, XIII).[31] How similar are the smooth lines of the back, and the groove of the backbone (cf. Pl. XLIV). How alike are the heavy legs, thighs, and buttocks (Pls. XIII, XLIII). Here one can see a similar female form translated into stone in a comparable fashion. Looking again at the Cyrene goddess, one perceives, particularly in the somewhat unrealistic firmness of the bust, that the type of naturalism it exemplifies is a little more abstract than it seems at first sight, an

impression equalled in a second look at the croucher, evident in the
Vienne-Louvre example (Pl. XIII). There is also a sharpness of treatment to both, suggesting that their originals were both bronze. Finally,
if the attempt to restore the bronze original of the crouching type with
an Eros is an accurate reconstruction,[32] this subsidiary mass, three-
quarters of the way toward the back of the principal volume, is matched
in the case of the standing figure by the draped dolphin, whose size
approximates that of the Eros. The two Aphrodites, both developed
three-dimensional conceptions in the full round, whose front and back
views are comparable, whose side views are simple geometrical shapes, a
cone and a cylinder, form an esthetic pair. Their ostensible differences of spatial organization are more than matched by other likenesses.

This attribution of the original of the Aphrodite _anadyomene_ to
around the middle of the third century B.C., or a decade or so later, on
account of its similarity to the sleeping satyr, makes it a near
contemporary of the half-draped creation, a reasonable conclusion. The
flatter, more open construction of the nude figure may indicate a somewhat later date, but like the famous sleeping satyr, it is at home in
the later 200's B.C. Both express an ideal of feminine beauty in
keeping with the fusion of genre charm and the traditional Greek respect
for the dignity and glory of the human body. Worthy successors to the
masterpieces of Praxiteles, they would have been strangely ill at ease
in that later time of passion, exaggeration, and Atticism which was the
Pergamene peak of Hellenistic sculpture, or its aftermath of classicism.

Such conclusions are echoed by Carpenter, except for his date for
the Cyrene figure, which is too late.[33]

"The marble Aphrodite of Cyrene in the Terme at Rome -- expertly
copied in late imperial Roman times from a Hellenistic bronze of
the third quarter of the third century B.C. -- embodies and
displays in exquisite perfection the deceptive simplicity of
pose, subtlety of surface and nonchalant ease of volume, which
characterize this phase of unexaggerated Naturalism. The nude
Praying Boy, once in Berlin, is almost a companion to the
Aphrodite.... We should at least understand it (the period)
well enough to see that it is out of its indrawn poses and direct
observation of nature that the crouching Aphrodite of Doidalsas
was created...."

### 3. Numismatic and Literary Evidence

Information derived from coins of Roman date can not be of direct
service in dating the two varieties of Aphrodite anadyomene, but does
indicate where they were well known. The half-draped figure is a relatively uncommon numismatic image. In an autonomous issue from Apameia
in Phrygia the goddess appears facing front, both hands to her hair, and
a nearly identical pose is employed on coins from Karallia in Isauria,
of Crispins, and Methana, Argolidis, on the Greek mainland.[34] As sometimes happens, the pose is a mirror image of the statue type, i.e., in
reverse, with the shoulders and arms ascending to the left. The two
relatively backward communities in Asia Minor were hardly places where

one might expect famous original work to have been produced. Karallia, Isauria, lay inland from Pamphylia, a territory which was under intermittent Ptolemaic control or influence, largely during the earlier third century B.C., and Arsinoë II as the wife of Lysimachus was a power in the area for a short time.[35] Any conclusions concerning the origins of the statue from these coins, especially the one from Argolidis, would be tenuous, but they at least do not rule out an Egyptian connection.

The situation is not so vague for the nude anadyomene. In the first place, there are at least twenty-two issues showing this version, revealing that it was the major type, and their distribution pattern recalls that of those coins depicting the crouching Aphrodite by Doidalsas of Bithynia, for both are centered in Northwest Asia Minor. Bernhart counted seven depicting the anadyomene from Bithynia, including four from Prusa and Olympum, to which should be added another in the collection of the American Numismatic Society, two from Caesarea Germanicopolis, and one from Nicaea.[36] Two of those from Prusa were minted under Trajan; the remainder are of the third century A.D. or autonomous.[37] The same author recorded six, dated primarily in the third century A.D., from Lydia, which is adjacent to Bithynia. Two of these came from Philadelphia, two from Saitta, and one each from Tralles, autonomous, and Bageis.[38] There are three autonomous issues from that portion of Phrygia to the East of Lydia, two from Laodikeia, and one from Peltai.[39] Finally there is one autonomous example from that universal center of Aphrodite worship, Aphrodisias in Caria, a city on whose coins many different images of the deity appear (Pl. XXV).[40]

It is significant that those issues of the mid-third century B.C. statue of the crouching Aphrodite type, traceable to Doidalsas of Bithynia on other grounds, show an almost identical chronological and geographical pattern of distribution.[41] One is led to believe from the coins alone that here too was the home of the nude anadyomene, and that the plastic image may also belong in the third century before Christ. When one takes into account the stylistic affinities of these types, they certainly appear to constitute two of a kind. The relatively greater number and more precise geographical limits of the issues showing the nude anadyomene support the thesis that it was the more famous example, and allow us to suspect, if we wish, that the other variety may not have originally been conceived as an Aphrodite.

Venerem lavantem se Daedalsas stantem Polycharmos, wrote Pliny in a confused and confusing passage (N.H. 36.36). Nearly a century ago it was suggested that the standing Venus was an anadyomene, a proposal that has been subsequently denied in order to give Polycharmus credit for the Aphrodite binding her sandal.[42] There does not yet exist enough evidence to decide.

CHAPTER IV


APHRODITE BINDING HER SANDAL:  A CREATION OF THE

MIDDLE HELLENISTIC AGE


One of the most numerous later Greek plastic versions of Aphrodite,
popularly known as the sandalbinder, exists today in many varied
statuettes of marble and bronze (Pls. XIV-XVIII, XXI-XXIV). Previous
periodic discussions of this intriguing type have yielded different and
even contradictory conclusions concerning its proper place within the
sequential development of Hellenistic sculpture.[1] One may find support
for assigning its creation to the circle of Lysippus, which was the
position of Furtwängler. More recent opinions have tended to evaluate
it as an expression of the artistic taste of Asia Minor toward the
middle of the second century B.C., a view first put forth by Klein and
adhered to by the Italian scholar Anti. It was subsequently opposed by
Pfuhl, who preferred to place it in the third. Bieber, who redefined
Klein's rococo as a pervasive mood, rather than as a manifestation of
the second century, included it as an example of rococo, and assigned
its origin to the circle of Alexandria, without any precise date. Thus,
to quote one of the reviewers of her Sculpture of the Hellenistic Age,
it became "the sandalbinder, split between Alexandria and Rococo."[2]

It is the purpose of this essay to examine and define the image against the background of Greek sculpture of the third and second centuries before Christ. After a synopsis of the problem, the type will be analyzed stylistically to determine the manner in which the original was conceived. In order to prove that replicas vary according to their own date, or, to quote the truism, "an artist must express his own time," a pair of Roman versions will be included, for their very differences enable us to visualize the Hellenistic specimens more clearly. A date late in the third century will be checked against other evidence, external and stylistic, followed by a study of the evolution of the type in the second century B.C., revealing the artistic characteristics of the late Hellenistic epoch, and showing why the inception of the figure of Aphrodite binding her sandal must be ascribed to an earlier period. Finally, an attribution to Asia Minor, aided by coins and terra-cottas, is secured by identifying a group as the work of the same artist.

## 1. Introduction

The most recent extended account of Aphrodite in the guise of a sandalbinder may well serve as a point of departure. On the occasion of the acquisition of a Roman bronze example by the Museo Civico in Padua (Pls. XVI, XVII), Anti discussed the type at length.[3] He took the opportunity to list the eighty-five replicas in sculpture then known to him, seven illustrations on gems or pastes, examples of five versions in terra cotta, and one on coins of Roman date from Aphrodisias in Caria.[4] It also appears on a coin of Apollonia in Mysia, which he was unable to verify.[5] Upon returning from a visit to Egypt, the Italian scholar

added four more and, since his list was drawn up in 1927, at least five

additional statuettes have been known.[6] The total for plastic examples

alone is thus ninety-five.

Following a classification according to type, Anti recorded two

principal varieties, and three minor ones, distinguished by overall pose

and the position of the right arm. Of the first, variant A, he counted

twenty-one specimens, made up of seventeen in marble, two in bronze, and

two miniatures in silver. Places of discovery extended to Rome and the

West, but it was notable that in the East only a few came from Greece,

and there was a marked concentration in Egypt.[7] It might have been

pointed out in this connection that the examples from Rome, which com-

prised the bulk of these from the Western Mediterranean, seem to date

from the imperial period. This group was distinguished from the other

versions in that the figure's left shoulder was advanced toward the

breast, and the left forearm was extended forward. Most of these

marbles have been broken since antiquity; those which have felt the

restorer's hand exhibit varying degrees of technical and imaginative

skill, rendering their study difficult but fascinating.[8]

Variant B was differentiated from A in that the right shoulder, the

statue's left, was held more in line with the torso, remaining more

horizontal, so that the composition appeared less closely massed, and,

in spite of the similar inclination of the torso, the body was less

twisted. Together with the nearly identical variant C, differing only in the position of the left arm, there were thirty-nine statuettes in this group, almost twice as many as in variant A. Whereas the figures in A were marble, thirty-two bronze and seven stone pieces made up variants B and C. Four of the marbles were suspect as erroneous restorations. Total geographical distribution was about equally divided, so that we may attach little significance to provenience.[9] Anti concluded his list with variants D and E, one bronze each, and two dozen unidentifiable specimens.[10] Overall, forty-three replicas came from the East, and twenty-eight from the West.

The conventional method of classification first adopted in Bernouilli's *Aphrodite* in 1873 revealed that there was a marble "Egyptian" group, variant A, and another one of bronze, variant B, but did not, as Anti recognized, take into account a number of variations. The degree to which the head was turned, changes in the attitude of the torso, the presence or absence of a supporting column, rudder, or Herm or Eros, all these were ignored. The Italian scholar reasoned logically that the conformation of a bronze original would have been closer to the commoner variant B, largely bronzes, whose more upright pose was better balanced, and that its scale would have been close to such works as the Pompeian dancing faun, 71 cm., or the Narcissus, 63 cm. Like Reinach before him, Anti looked to Asia Minor for the original, on the basis of coins and terra cottas, suggested one Polycharmos as the artist, and the second century B.C. as the time.[11]

Two examples of the sandalbinder in the British Museum are replicas of a bronze original.[12] One from Paramythia is reliable with respect to every portion but the lower legs (Pl. XV). Yet the knees were complete, permitting a nineteenth century restoration of respectable accuracy and discretion, in which the right arm was left unrestored. Its height of 20 cm., or 6-7/8 inches, is representative of the smaller versions. The other was said to have been found near Patras, perhaps at Olympia (Pl. XIV).[13] Although the arms and part of the torso at the waistline have not survived, the position of both legs remains clear. Standing 54 cm., or 21-1/2 inches, in height, it may have depicted the original scale.

## 2. Stylistic Analysis of Several Replicas

When viewed from the front, the central volume of the statuette of Aphrodite binding her sandal rests jointly upon her crossed left leg and the support of the right (Pl. XV). Seen from the side, the firm curve of the buttocks and the graceful arch of the shoulders effectively bind the figure, as seen in the example from Patras (Pl. XIV). The total shape is clearest from the side where the whole body resembles a triangle on the pillar of the leg, with the head moved subtly off its peak. From the front, the head rests on the curve of the shoulders. Attached to this curve is the extended left arm, whose function is that of a separate balancing device to prevent the figure from toppling, even though it originally had a support. Its outline clearly, indeed, almost too obviously, would have matched that of the left leg, for compositional lines extended from both came perilously close to being identical and transforming the statue into a static mass. Refinements of contour prevent this from happening, however, and maintain a sense of temporarily arrested motion. That such an effect is vibrant in its tenseness is due to the support below the torso's compact form. The slim line of the figure's leg tapers down to a thin ankle while, from thigh to knee, the "V" shape of the outline of both legs serves to cradle the torso above. Taken together, these two elements of the composition may be compared to the outline of a vase with a flared top. These supporting parts flow smoothly into the torso, while the vertical right arm serves as a reinforcing accent, linked with the left leg when the statue is seen in profile, or with the right from a frontal vantage point. The head of the goddess caps the various volumes and outlines of her figure. The artist who created this type turned the head to the right, opening up the form and psychologically avoiding a direct contact between Aphrodite and the observer. Formally, the outward turn of the head provides a nice balance to the extended left arm and partially open hand, for head and hand are precisely opposite each other at the same level. In the statuette from Paramythia (Pl. XV) this counterpoint was so artfully contrived that even the line of the gaze, out and down, was equated with the inclination and direction of the left forefinger. Just as the form was slim and compressed at its base, so is it broad and expansive at its top.

A Roman statuette in Padua (Pls. XVI, XVII), which inspired the study by the Italian scholar Anti, was dated by him to the second

century A.D.[14] Thus to call it a copy should be done advisedly, for a
close inspection reveals it to be more nearly an adaptation. Not only
are details changed, such as the hair with its flowing locks, but there
are also adjustments in the pose. The angle of the upper left leg is a
trifle above the horizontal, the lower part is less canted, and the
thrust of the arm down to the sandal really commences at the neck, and
continues an anchor-shaped profile which begins with the other arm. The
head is more sharply inclined to concentrate specifically on the task of
binding her sandal. With the loss of the distinctly delineated waistline, the clear interrelatedness of the parts of the body has disappeared.    Seen frontally, there is a smooth flow down to a much narrower
cone below the torso due to the slimmer angle of the legs. The reduced
volume was complemented by the thin support under the outstretched arm.
In sum, the later reproduction is not articulated in the same manner,
but has exchanged a developed plastic sense for an equally valid but
different pictorial one, and hence is no longer the same kind of formal
study. Its shift in emphasis has made it more illusionistic, for the
surface changes more evenly all the way around as one view merges into
the next. It is hardly surprising that these differences encompass some
of the features we think of when contrasting Roman art to Greek.

How completely another artist of Roman times has transformed,
ignored, or misunderstood the composition of the delicately poised
figure! A third version in the British Museum has so altered pose, gaze,
and gesture that the now cluttered image has changed its character

(Pl. XVIII).[15] By varying the position of the upraised leg and by straighten-
ing the torso, the composition has been transformed into a more open one,
while a conch-shell rim of drapery, soaring like a banner on high,
destroys what once was a graceful and complex counterpoint. The gaze is
now direct, and the gesture mechanical, as the statue rests, permanent
and immobile, upon an already overloaded prop. The high base with its
carved steps elevates the type of Aphrodite binding her sandal to the
status of a cult statue, when in actuality this kind of image was more
probably a humbler votive offering.

Yet it is important to look carefully at this image. Like the
other examples, this one did more than recall an original creation out
of past time, proving that its message was still valid, and certainly it
must be considered in its own context to be understood properly. The
more upright pose introduces a new element, for this figure is arranged
in vertical planes rather than by the volumes which, at an earlier time,
defined the relationship between the form and the surrounding space.
The principal plane is, of course, that set forth by the torso and
supporting leg. From it, the head projects only slightly forward, and
its depth is measured by the thickness of the drapery with its irregular
border. Before its thin, slablike conformation we can distinguish
another plane, established by the upraised knee. The shinbone reveals
that this forward boundary of the figure is actually a diagonal bar,
defined by the hands of the goddess. In keeping with this novel compositional construction for the sandalbinder, Aphrodite's right forearm

is strangely flat, and the fingers have been splayed sideways. The shallowly-cut little steps, each of whose risers echoes one of the planes of the figure, help to set it in a pose of fixed frontality, whose hieratic quality is as distinctive an expression of the late antique as is the upward cast of the glance. Thus the copies vary according to the dates at which they were made.

Did the image of Aphrodite binding her sandal have a support as originally conceived? Most of the marble examples, like the statue in the Arenberg collection, needed one for stability (Pl. XXI).[16] As a matter of fact, the bronze versions which have been considered, even the Paramythia and Patras pieces, appear to have been completed with some kind of pillar.[17] A coin of Roman date from Aphrodisias shows a short column, knee high, with an Eros perched on top, beneath a crescent moon (Pl. XXV).[18] Many of the gems, which date likewise from the imperial age, show assorted types of supports.[19] In the classical period, Praxiteles incorporated supporting devices into his compositions, as in the Hermes and Dionysus from Olympia, and a post-Praxitelean small bronze in Dresden is inconceivable in its leaning pose without some sort of support.[20] In addition, from a practical point of view, no matter how wildly impractical we may imagine the Greeks to have been, to suppose that the original had a support is reasonable from the point of view of stability, although the weight-bearing leg could well have been anchored. Nor is it irrelevant to bring up the basic fact that in order to balance in the sandalbinder's pose the weight-bearing foot must be directly beneath the neck. Yet this foot and leg, rather than being inclined inward, are aligned vertically in several reliable and unrestored Hellenistic replicas, such as the Patras bronze (Pl. XIV), or the Arenberg marble (Pl. XXI). Finally, the fact that an overwhelming majority of the copies employed one proves that the figure was customarily conceived with a supporting bracket.

### 3. Dating the Sandalbinder

The motif of binding one's sandal did not originate with the creation of this type of Aphrodite. It can be seen in the gesture of a Nike on the parapet of the temple of Athena Nike erected on the Acropolis in Athens at the end of the fifth century B.C.[21] The figure, in high relief, bends forward with her right arm extended to the right sandal, but her left foot is merely drawn up, not crossed over the opposite leg as in the case of the sandalbinder. The Nike wears diaphanous drapery so that the outline of the body may be perceived clearly. Since we are dealing here with relief sculpture, and the figure is ordered more or less frontally, the Nike appears to be leaning against a wall, and was not intended to be conceived as freestanding.

By the mid-fourth century the same theme was used for a divinity and in conjunction with a figure in the round. The Lansdowne statue of Hermes binding his sandal, now in the Ny Carlsberg Glyptothek in Copenhagen, is a work associated with Lysippus and is properly to be identified as Hermes, the messenger of the gods (Pl. XIX).[22] Except for a cloak hanging from the left arm, the figure is nude. Unlike the expansive quality of the Nike on the parapet, the form of this statue is compressed and tightly knit. As Hermes bends forward to reach down with his right hand to the right sandal, he has drawn up his right foot and placed it on a rock. Meanwhile, he rests his left arm across his up-raised right knee, with the hand toward his right. At the same time he looks off to the left. Thus arms, legs, and gaze crisscross in front of the bent figure. The composition revolves around and over the vertical pillar of the right leg, reinforced by the parallel right arm, and the long, slim forms are caught in a momentary attitude. The Hermes, as well as that other Lysippan statue, the Apoxyomenos,[23] reveals as its most essential conception an understanding of how to expand into the surrounding space without loss of plastic unity, in order to create a fully three-dimensional work.

The Tyche of Antioch, a renowned statue by Eutychides, a pupil of Lysippus, helps to establish more precisely the artistic milieu neces-sary for the creation of Aphrodite binding her sandal. It has been dated to around 296-293 B.C., on the evidence of Pliny (N.H. 34.51). The full-size marble version in the Vatican and a bronze statuette in the Metropolitan Museum of Art in New York show a seated, draped, female figure with her right leg crossed over the left (Pl. IV).[24] The left arm beneath her garment is out to one side, resting on the rock on which she sits, and the other is propped on the right leg, elbow bent sharply so that her forearm and hand point to her face. In the Vatican example her right foot is supported by a personification of the Orontes river,

represented swimming. Her gaze to the right opposes that of the Tyche.
Her composition overall resembles a one-sided diamond, or a triangle on
its side, with the apex pointing to her left. Across its surface the
patterns of the drapery set up a complicated net of interweaving lines,
while the limbs of the figure establish spatial relations in front and
to one side, as is true of the sandalbinder. With the Tyche, the linear
expansion into space initiated by Lysippus has been adopted and adapted
for the definition of triangular planes.

Another composition of the third century is closer to the Aphrodite
binding her sandal in its momentary pose, and its naturalistic rendition
of the figure. The crouching Aphrodite not only depicts the identical
goddess in the nude, but, more importantly, is datable to around 250
B.C.[25] While it continues the Praxitelean tradition of representing
Aphrodite at her bath, she is envisaged in the actual act of bathing, in
a kneeling posture whose temporary nature recalls the sandalbinder
(Pls. IX, X, XII, XIII). Hence these two are alike in their revelation of
the sculptor's awareness of time, as well as in the choice of a genre subject. In both respects she is removed from a timeless, divine realm and
conceived as existing more in a mundane, mortal sphere. Furthermore,
the poses of the crouching and the sandalbinding Aphrodite exhibit
strong parallels in their anatomical display of the female form. Both
have a gently curving back whose parabolic line bounds one side of the
volume of the composition. By arranging one or both of the lower limbs
approximately at right angles, the contour of the buttocks becomes

closely similar for both figures. The firmness of their binding,
defining curves represents a Hellenistic application to the female form
of the principles of refinement worked out by the bronzecasters of the
fourth century B.C., who, headed by Lysippus, modified the kouroi tradition. Perhaps our awareness of the balance between naturalism and
abstraction possessed by these two figures of Aphrodite may be made more
specific by recalling the soft, plump fullness of the Aphrodite of
Syracuse.[26] Its famous voluptuous character, so perilously close to
eroticism, displays a creative vision far different from the taut,
tactile sense of the mid-third century.

Alike in their sense of time, their type of naturalism, and plastic
conception, these two images are nevertheless different in the effect
produced by their total three-dimensional composition. In spite of the
similar forward inclination of the torso, the part played by the arms in
the case of the sandalbinder has a tendency to open up the volume and
expand the figure into the surrounding space. The crouching figure, on
the other hand, is indifferent to or even repels everything outside herself, being withdrawn into an almost perfect pyramidal composition.
After 250 B.C., in the sequence of heroic groups, the volume becomes
more expansive, from the Menelaus and Patroclus monument through the
Gallic groups of Pergamon.[27] Their themes and pathos are rather remote
from the sandalbinder's less grandiloquent scale and artistic expression.
The Aphrodite binding her sandal can be roughly matched in size and
absence of deep seriousness if we consider the boy strangling a goose of

Boethos, whose blocklike solidity and theme of desperate struggle echoes and parodies the Pergamene dedications which it must have followed.[28] The early second century B.C., the apparent date of Boethos' creation, may be tentatively established as a _terminus ante quem_, just as that of the crouching Aphrodite of Doidalsas furnishes a _terminus post quem_.

Pfuhl substantiated this conclusion when he placed the Patras example of the sandalbinder (Pl. XIV) in the second half of the third century because its coiffure, especially in the curve of the locks in front of the ears, was close to that of Arsinoë III, queen of Egypt from 222 to 209 B.C. (Pl. XX).[29] In addition, the marble replicas making up the group known as variant A came predominantly from Egypt. If, still thinking in terms of the second half of the century, we consider a representative statue from this group, we find further support for assigning the sandalbinder to this period.

A headless, though handsome, marble example of the Aphrodite from Egypt belonged to the collection in the Arenberg Palace, Brussels, in 1903 (Pl. XXI).[30] Supposedly from Alexandria, at 67 cm. it corresponds with the scale suggested for the original, and typical of variant A, the left shoulder is advanced more toward the breast. Two aspects of this figure are notable. The slim proportions of the torso echo very distinctly those of the Patras piece, and the long curve of the rounded back and firmness of the buttocks recall the anatomical proportions of the crouching Aphrodite. This marble, then, continues the application of Lysippic features of harmony to the female figure and repeats again

the formal conceptions of feminine anatomy known to be expressive of the
mid-third century B.C.  Nevertheless, the sandalbinder's interrelation-
ships between form and space are more characteristic of the period after
250 B.C. than before that date.

### 4.  Egypt, Home of the First Adaptation

Recently, Bieber referred to the sandalbinder as follows:  "The
type of Aphrodite lifting her left foot and stooping down to unfasten
her sandal, so frequent in Asia Minor and the islands, is also found in
Alexandrian art; it is appropriate to this art circle.  A bronze
statuette in the Louvre from Tell-Ramses, near Damanhur, a terra-cotta
figurine, and a small marble torso, both in the Metropolitan Museum of
Art in New York, well show the complicated and elegant movements."[31]
It is only fair to point out that these examples upon which her wary
assertion that the original may belong to Alexandria was based include
a unique adaptation.  The bronze in the Louvre is the only one out of
the ninety-odd copies whose left forearm goes up, and has been classified traditionally all by itself as variant D.[32]  Unfortunately, to
locate the origin of this Aphrodite type in the land of the Ptolemies
does not seem a very likely possibility.  Numerous specimens of the
sandalbinder have been found in Egypt, but the principal evidence
against placing the creation of the image there lies in the technique
and stylistic character of these very examples.  On the other hand,
there can be little doubt that the first modification of the type
occurred in that country.

Only one of the bronze versions of the goddess known as variant B, typified by the Paramythia Patras pair, has been found in the country, while a disproportionately large number of copies of variant A are said to be Egyptian.[33] For the most part, they seem to be rather mediocre marble statues, which are difficult to study and identify with respect to date, but the bulk of the marble pieces exhibit a close uniformity in design. The Arenberg Aphrodite is exceptional due to its size, quality and similarity to the bronzes (Pl. XXI). We may contrast it with the far more characteristic fragmentary marble in the Cairo Museum (Pl. XXIII, No. 27456).[34] The difference is instantly apparent, for, even though the latter has been labelled variant B, its right shoulder is angled forward and down, rather than extended outward in a more horizontal direction. It is clear too that the traditional division between variants A and B omits one notable contrast, occurring in the position of the torso, which is strongly twisted on its axis so that the upper part is turned violently counterclockwise as Aphrodite stoops down toward her sandal. Compared to the statues from Paramythia (Pl. XV), or Patras (Pl. XIV), or even the Arenberg collection marble from Alexandria (Pl. XXI), with their effect of temporarily arrested motion, this one is actually moving, a difference so strong that it almost produces another variant. Behind it lies a major shift in conception. Imagine the marble in Cairo as a complete piece instead of being only a torso with broad hips and richly convex stomach. It then becomes a minor monument whose nature is unmistakably "baroque."

The pronounced features of the Egyptian type of the sandalbinder
are not equalled until the last quarter of the third century B.C.  At
that time in Asia Minor, as we have noted, a style employing powerful,
blocklike figures, working toward a close fidelity to nature, and marked
by strong twists of forms in space had reached its peak preparatory to
the culmination of Hellenistic sculpture in the heroic expansion of the
Pergamon altar.  To find kindred works from Egypt, distinguished by the
same solidity of volume but enlivened by the same tension-producing
twist as in the Cairo statuette, it is necessary to look to the very end
of the third century.  A masterpiece in this style, which is also a
female figure, makes a very apt contrast with the Aphrodite because it
has been attributed successfully to Alexandria itself.  It is the
statuette of a dancer in the Baker collection in New York.[35]  The bronze,
20.7 cm. high, is a study in the full round of a moving figure, whose
form is organized around a spiral.  Within this spiral the body exists
as a solid core for the volume on a broad base.  From the surface of the
statue project triangular forms as the dancer, tightly draped, veiled,
and covered with a voluminous but transparent mantle, swirls in a
pirouette.  The sculpture testifies to the development of an increasing
desire and ability on the part of artists of the period to represent the
energy of motion without loss of plastic unity, but rather with an
astonishingly contemporary third-dimensional sense.  The sandalbinder in
Egypt has been clearly affected by such studies of the dynamics of the
human body in action.  Her design, however, remains composed essentially
from the front and sides, for, no matter how admirably the back may have

been carved, it was conceived primarily with a profile view in mind.
The frontal vantage point displays a stomach of Oriental opulence, and
new proportions overall, expressing the artistic vernacular prevalent
throughout the Hellenistic world just before the pathetic exaggeration
and grandeur of Pergamene inspiration. Preserving some of the heaviness
and solidity characteristic of mid-century work and some of the spiralling torsion motivating later products, her more ample form became more
positively stooped, more definitely twisted, in short, more nearly in
motion. In accordance with the taste of a later time, a not dissimilar
change took place in another locally produced plastic type of the goddess, today in the Cairo Museum (Pl. XXII, No. 27457).[36] It depicts a
figure derived from the Knidian Aphrodite of Praxiteles, whose back
arches forward in a long convex curve, like a late Hellenistic modification of the same original in New York (Pl. II).[37] These examples,
transplanted, were transformed.

The typical marble image of Aphrodite binding her sandal, traceable
to Egypt, illustrates an adaptation of the original version which can
also be found there. Compared to the prototype, it is comprehensible
only as an intensified, later conception, whose closest parallels belong
at the end of the third century. Hence we may assign its development to
the decades beginning or ending with the year 200 B.C., and it reinforces our contention, drawn from stylistic evidence, that the original,
created after 250 B.C., was in existence before the end of the century.[38]

### 5. Later Development

During the latter half of the middle Hellenistic period a preference developed for extravagant scenic effects within sharply defined
limits, a tendency which had already commenced in the graceful artificiality of the elongated, twisted form of the sleeping Hermaphrodite, or
the equally patent unreality of the series of transparently draped
ladies extending from the late third century on.[39] The new standards
apply to an original mid-century marble of the Aphrodite type next in
the sequence. From the Sabouroff collection, it is now in Berlin (Pl.
XXIII).[40] Its high-piled, high-fashion coiffure revives one of the
fussier preferences of the post-Praxitelean decades.[41] We need not rely
upon stylistic chronological evidence derived from the sandalbinder
alone, for this statue has a support in the form of Priapus, of a type
common in the later Hellenistic age, when the crude fertility god from
Lampsacus came to be rather humorously regarded.[42]

The formal construction of this adaptation of the sandalbinder has
lost the pleasing rhythms expressed by the earlier examples. The nearly
impossible position of the head, chin jutting over the shoulder, dis-
closes that in this replica the decorative instinct has triumphed over
the previous balance between naturalism and convention. The demands of
harmony in this period were not concerned with bodily limitations.
Therefore the inharmonious mismatch of the torso, whose upper and lower
parts look as if they had been too tightly screwed together, is consistently in line with the times. For this contortion quickly generates an

energy which is dissipated almost as rapidly by the open forms of the elevated head, the arm which has been flung out, and the lifted, awkwardly canted head. The flow of the various parts of the body, which was typical of the more integrated earlier concepts, has given way to a lack of fusion, and the figure owes such appeal as it possesses to the extroverted vigor of its expression.

Another example, once in the Ccok Collection, carries this evolution further (Pl. XXIV, left).[43] Like the foregoing, it is marble, but the treatment is very different, for the modelling is carried through in a soft sfumato characteristic of Rhodian work before 100 B.C. The manner is not original, but is in line with the revival and reworking of the sculpture of the fourth century, as in the Venus of Melos (Pl. LII); the style of this specimen goes back to works like the girl from Chios in Boston.[44] Only the head and torso of this sandalbinder are original; the restoration shows her washing her foot. The head, contrasted to the one from Chios, lacks substance. Its excessive softness makes it a genuine companion-piece to another contemporary adaptation of a third-century statue of Aphrodite, the crouching type, confused with the anadyomene motif, found in Rhodes (Pl. XXI, Bottom).[45] These two eclectic examples from the first classical revival in history display a number of other similar traits, the chief among them being a flatness and diminished sense of volume. Their cross sections are exceptionally thin from front to back, but broader from side to side. Such sculpture was fitting in an age whose enjoyment of atmospheric pictorialism was making the principles of the painter's art steadily more predominant.

6. On the Location of the Type

Having furnished an answer to the question of the origin and evolution in time of the Aphrodite binding her sandal, it is relevant now to discuss its provenience. One can cite numismatics, for the sandalbinder was one of the many statues commemorated among the issues of Aphrodisias, appearing there once, along with the far commoner archaizing image of the goddess (Pl. XXV).[46] It appeared twice on issues of Apollonia in Mysia.[47] In this case, however, stronger evidence in favor of locating the original in Asia Minor is derived from representations of Aphrodite binding her sandal in terra-cotta. An example in Boston is one of a number of pieces depicting the goddess in that medium (Pl. XXVI).[48] It comes from Smyrna, a town on the northern half of the coast of Asia Minor, at the head of the road to Myrina and Pergamon. There are other similar works, some of which were manufactured with a support to produce a more stable object, but many of those previously classified as examples of the type are not really relevant, for some are draped modifications, and with others a foot which barely clears the ground constitutes the only common denominator.[49] If these are removed from consideration, it becomes evident that genuine specimens were commonest at Myrina.[50] The terra-cottas from this city between Smyrna and Pergamon have been studied as a group, and the examples of the sandalbinder from the cemetery there should be dated after the third century B.C., probably in the second, which accords perfectly well with our chronology.[51]

On the other hand, the production of terra-cottas elsewhere does not feature our type of Aphrodite. At Tanagra, the most famous center of the art of the coroplast, where production commenced in the decade between 340 and 330 B.C., and reached its peak during the third century, but continued thereafter, the sandalbinder was not a part of the repertoire.[52] Scattered finds included one example from Priene, a late one, datable to around 125 B.C.[53] Another came from Philadelphia, a city in Lydia founded by the Pergamene king Attalus II Philadelphus (159-138 B.C.) near a pass leading to the valley of the Maeander.[54] A third listed Tripoli as its provenience.[55] It is exceptionally significant that Egypt, a regular center of terra cotta production, can not be mentioned as the site of discoveries of the type in this material. Even Egyptian molds for making terra-cottas, which were very common and included such well known original Hellenistic figures as the Aphrodite Anadyomene (Pl. XLVII), have shown no record of the sandalbinder there.[56]

The distribution pattern of the local terra-cotta replicas is admissible as valid evidence for centering the Aphrodite binding her sandal in Asia Minor, particularly when combined with the absence of finds from a known center like Egypt, where many terra-cottas have been preserved. The range of figurines from Myrina embraced a wide variety of subjects, but among their reproductions of major works of Hellenistic sculpture we may note that another Aphrodite was paired with the sandalbinder, the crouching type.[57] This figure, already frequently referred to as another original of the third century B.C., in connection with the artistic analysis, with reference to the date of the sandalbinder, and also as a comparable example in the case of the numismatic images, we know existed in the original in the same general area.  If a case for the location of our figure, paralleling that of the crouching goddess in so many ways, leads toward a consideration of the north central coastal region of Asia Minor, then we should hunt for any further evidence there, in the form of corresponding pieces of sculpture.

## 7.  Stylistic Correspondence with Other Works

The art of the northwestern quarter of Asia Minor was dominated by the subject preference and patronage of Pergamon during the period to which we have assigned the original of the Aphrodite binding her sandal. Toward the end of the century there we find that the memory of the desparate campaigns against the Gauls, already commemorated by the large dedicatory group in the capital city, led to another group in Athens, less than life size.  Their reduced scale hardly makes them the equivalent, however, of the sandalbinder, although their use in combination of outwardly opening forms and a kneeling figure with upturned head, as in the Persian soldier, shows the same mixed tendencies visible in the sandalbinder.[58]  Examples more comparable to her are encountered when we turn to a group of satyrs found in or associated with Pergamon.  A youthful, jolly, nude satyr, now in Berlin, who seems about to turn to his left, exhibits a twist in the trunk of his body like the Aphrodite, and his head is also turned in the opposite direction.[59]  One arm is crooked up and over his head, and his other holds an animal skin, while his pipes are in his hand. Another, which came from a ship sunk off Mahdia, is running, arms outstretched, head bent up and body inclined forward (Pl. XXVII).[60] A third representative of his breed, carrying two torches, stands still, holding one torch in his left hand above his head, and the other at his side (Pl. XXVII).[61] Finally, a splendid example, unfortunately armless, and like the previous one, in New York, stands on his left leg and raises the right, as if about to dance (Pl. XXVX).[62] As he bends forward, slightly twisted, his conformation, especially in the torso, strongly resembles that of the sandalbinder.

A known work from this region consists of the Invitation to the Dance group from Cyzicus, with its satyr and nymph. The latter (Pls. XXXIII-XXXIV) is notable for its resemblance to the Patras figure's head (Pl. XIV), and to the coiffure of Arsinoë III (Pl. XX), because it too displays a small forelock of hair in front of the ear. The group, datable to early in the second century B.C., was reconstructed by Klein on the basis of a coin from Cyzicus, using bodies of a satyr in Florence, a nymph in Brussels, and a pair of heads in Venice (Pls. XXXIX-XXXIV).[63] There are many resemblances between the body and motif of the marble nymph and the Paramythia bronze (Pls. XV, XXX, XXXI). The fact that both are copies argues for caution, yet their common characteristics substantiate their association. More than the gesture of raising the left leg to attend to a sandal with the right hand, which, in the case of the nymph, represents the last gasp of the habit of working in triangular forms so popular in the third century, the treatment of the upper

half of the torso unites these two. A similar inclination forward, with
the same downward emphasis on the right side, is almost identical. Even
though the placement of the left arm differs, note that the curving
contour of the shoulders, particularly evident in the Brussels version
of the nymph, matches the same line on the Paramythia figure so closely
that it seems as if it could only have been transposed. The artists of
the Paramythia bronze and the nymph in Florence, in each case, modelled
the female bust, stomach, indented waistline, and rounded abdomen in an
identical manner.

Similarities between the two female heads are less readily apparent,
but equally convincing. The nymph of Venice, with her high-style hairdo
(Pls. XXXIII-XXXIV), not only duplicates the same semi-circular tendrils
which adorn the temples and forehead of the Paramythia face (Pl. XV).
Below, in both instances, the lines of the eyebrows are clearly marked
over large eyes set wide apart, and the same formula is applied to the
straight noses, and modest-sized mouths, with small lips. In neither
case is there any sense of harshness or angularity; instead, the changing
curves are gentle yet definite, and when one looks at the head of the
Patras figure (Pl. XIV), an original of the period, one is struck by the
same soft handling of the features as in the nymph, which come through
in spite of the fact that the latter is a Roman copy. At the back of
each head the hair is gathered up by the same kind of chignon, placed at
precisely the same spot. A terpsichorean nymph, unlike the goddess
Aphrodite, was not entitled to display a diadem or sphendone. Lastly,

although Klein united the Venice head, which had been broken at the neck, with the body of a nymph whose existing head and neck did not belong, we have no cause to disagree with his careful placement of it, so that she glanced out to her left. She did not need to look to the trivial task of fiddling with the straps of her sandal any more than did the Aphrodite, who also looked away to her left. The gaze of the nymph thus is directed not only out over her hand and sandal, including that part of the composition psychologically, but also upward to her companion the satyr. Traces of the pupils of her eyes are still visible on the Venice face. The angle of her head helps to open up the form and is consistent with the rest of her figure, which shows a further development in this direction than the sandalbinder, which, on other grounds, has already been dated earlier. It is remarkable that two replicas should persist in such a close degree of correspondence. They furnish abundant grounds for the inescapable conclusion that their originals were made by the same artist.

## 8. Attribution to an Artist

It is possible that the name of Polycharmos may be associated with the Aphrodite binding her sandal on the basis of an obscure passage in Pliny (<u>N.H.</u> 36.3.6), <u>Venerem levantem se sedaedalsas stantem Polycharmus</u>. It is a confused reference, and different manuscripts give different readings, as quoted by Jex-Blake and Sellers, but all alike assert next that Polycharmos was the author of a standing Venus.[64] The first part of the phrase in the text has been taken by Theodore Reinach to refer to the figure of the crouching Aphrodite by Doidalsas of Bithynia, an interpretation which has met with general acceptance.[65] The fact that the statement of Pliny forms part of his account of sculpture in marble need not force us to believe that the originals must have been of this material, rather than bronze, because the examples he describes in the early imperial period may well have been copies.[66] Salomon Reinach has also compared the various versions of the last line quoted here and was led to connect Polycharmos with the statue type of Aphrodite binding her sandal, and to identify him as its creator.[67] To Venerem...stantem Polycharmus he would add the phrase pede in uno. His ingenious inference is based on three contentions. First, the phrase "a standing Venus by Polycharmos" is confusing if not meaningless in its extant form, for it does not differentiate the figure from any of the numerous other standing examples which have survived. Second, to suppose that Pliny erred in his compilation at this point, or that his source was incomplete is not beyond the realm of possibility. Third, the text itself varies, proving that the copyists were baffled, and yet every one of the surviving manuscripts reports that the Venus of Polycharmos was standing. Therefore, we can infer that the phrase was obscure originally because of an omission in the text, and one is justified in making a brief, simple addition. Whether Reinach's pede in uno corresponds precisely to what was left out or not we have no way of ascertaining, but his suggestion is clear and sensible. Why should mention have been made, in the case of this particular statue alone, out of the multitude cited by the

indefatigable Pliny, that it stands, unless there were something
distinctive about such a pose?

One must, unfortunately, counter this proposal with another, for
it has also been suggested that Pliny meant the type known as Aphrodite
anadyomene.[68] In the present state of our knowledge, it must be
admitted that the anadyomene, a famous version of the goddess of
antiquity, has at least an equal claim, and that it requires no emendation or addition to the text. Regardless of who the artist may have
been, should the foregoing attribution of the group known as the Invitation to the Dance be accepted, then the author of both it and the
Aphrodite who binds her sandal acquires thereby a more positive identity
and even a certain stature.

CHAPTER V

THE CLIMAX AND AFTERMATH OF HELLENISTIC SCULPTURE

SEEN IN NEW AND OLD IDEALS OF APHRODITE

In contrast to all earlier Greek art, that of the end of the middle
Hellenistic epoch and of the late period is characterized by multiplicity, variety and eclecticism. One can not follow a method of examining
one type as the most characteristic representation and thereby interpret
these phases of Hellenistic sculpture. In the first place, standards in
art changed at a much more rapid pace as the second and first centuries
B.C. witnessed what might be called a cultural speedup, or, in dramatic
terms, a dénouement, albeit in a highly individual fashion. An increasing awareness of time, a liking for momentary or more active poses, and
the depiction of figures caught in ever briefer instants, which could be
seen at the end of the third century B.C. in the development of the
Aphrodite binding her sandal, is a not unrelated phenomenon. Secondly,
the attentions of sculptors and the desires of their patrons were
diverted toward the hitherto unsuspected effects obtainable by the re-
elaboration of types previously established to make them more appealing
to contemporary taste. Hence there is no one new type of Aphrodite in
sculpture which can represent this experimental period, and what is
really novel is the way in which older images were seen and conceived.

It is important to note that the same inability to unite which
plagued the classic Greek political units affected the Hellenistic kingdoms, and, enfeebled by wars among themselves, during these last
centuries before Christ one after another was annexed by Rome.  Greece
came under direct control with the sack of Corinth in 146 B.C.; Pergamon
was willed to the Roman State by its last king, who died in 133 B.C.;
Cyrene, 96, Syria, 65, and Egypt, 30, all succumbed during the first
century.  That this loss of independence led men to look with longing at
the past can be seen through the art produced, and also by recalling
Pliny (N.H. 34.52), who, in his book on bronze sculpture, stated that a
revival, apparently of classical, archaizing, and even early Hellenistic
subjects and styles got under way in 156-152 B.C.[1]  It had of course
been presaged by the earlier admiration at Pergamon of the Attic works
of the fifth century before Christ.  In view of these momentous changes,
one may recall the label, "Graeco-Roman," once applied to the years
between 146 and 30 B.C.[2]  Actually, however, the major artistic activity
was still Greek, and the simpler convention of Late Hellenistic emphasizes this age of mixed tendencies more accurately as the final period
of Greek sculpture.

### 1.  Originality and Atticism

The period covering the century between 200 and 100 B.C. and the
following decade is extraordinarily diverse in terms of the multiplica-
tion of images of Aphrodite, yet the following scheme may describe with
some logic the shifting standards of this 110-year span, derivable from

the shifting Aphrodite ideal. By these changes, the period can be
divided into two parts, based upon datable works. Each period harks
back to earlier concepts, but establishes a different relationship to
the past. The first phase exhibits a preference for large-scale figures,
and a new awareness of the basic plastic forms of the late fourth century B.C., unlike the mid-third century, whose crouching Aphrodite was
derived in part from vase painting,[3] as seems to have been the case with
the Aphrodite anadyomene.[4] The second commences around 150 B.C. with
elaborate adaptations, but soon shifts to a more imitative reconstruction of known types, distinguished by contemporary standards of rhythm
and harmony. A third period, definable as neo-classic, grows out of the
second during the last third of the second century B.C. and extends into
the first.

In the earliest phase belongs the Capitoline Aphrodite (Pl. XXXVI),
apparently a product of Asia Minor shortly after 200 B.C., a reworking
of the Medici type (Pl. III).[5] Praxiteles, with his renowned marble
nude Aphrodite of Cnidos (cf. Pl. II), is of course the prototype for
both. The fourth century master had conceived of the goddess as laying
aside her last article of clothing, which she still retained in her left
hand, with most of her garment draped over a tall water vase, a loutrophoros, used in a pre-nuptial ritual bath. Her gentle gaze was directed
to her left, and her right hand was placed modestly before her bust as
if anticipating an invasion of her privacy. In the Capitoline figure,
the same ritual vase is at the same left side of the statue, where it

helps support the marble image, and over it lies a garment whose edges
are bound with a rich decorative fringe. Another copy of the Capitoline
image in the Louvre shows an Eros on a dolphin at the left side.[6] The
dolphin and Eros look like copyists' additions, but other works from the
third century on use a fringed cloak, such as the bronze Alexandrian
dancer in the Baker collection, or the "Pudicitia" type as seen in the
Louvre and Ashmolean versions.[7] The fringed costume reinforces the
dating posited above.

As an example of the early second century B.C., it is significant
also in its obvious similarity to the Medici Aphrodite (Pl. III). Like
the latter, the Capitoline holds nothing in her hands, so that the only
excuse for their position is the specific one of covering her nakedness,
a motive which in both cases draws attention to the female attributes,
and the position of the Capitoline s right hand is such that the breasts
are revealed rather than concealed. Thus the barrier she rather ineffec-
tually establishes becomes a transparent invitation to look beyond. The
importance of this point is more formal than psychological, however.

In this work appears a factor new to traditional Greek sculpture.
During the late Hellenistic age, starting in the first half of the
second century B.C., there developed a type of composition displaying a
strong sense of two-dimensionality when seen from the side, in conjunction with a strong feeling for depth and existence in space when seen
from the front. This deliberate and peculiar combination is best known
in the so-called one-view or einansichtige groups.[8] It replaces the

traditional neutral sense of space in Greek art, gone forever after the latter's logical and inevitable culmination in the solid and unyielding background of the large frieze at Pergamon.[9] In relief, where it is easier to measure degrees of spatial depth, one can see from the very great projection of the gods and giants how forbiddingly the background plane was regarded. The later, smaller, narrative frieze of Telephus from the great altar is the first datable Greek work to exhibit a positive spatial sense, for the wall plane has suddenly become a transparent veil whose capacity to represent a continuous vista was here cautiously but definably exploited.[10]

The Aphrodite of the Capitoline Museum (Pl. XXXVI) displays a different but complementary expression of the same space concept in terms of the plane before the body; it reveals the same urge to set up and then pierce through a foreground as was evident in the case of the Telephus frieze, where layers of depth were also established through the arrangement of the figures and by other devices. If this hypothesis should not be accepted, then the Capitoline statue, expertly analyzed by Sir Kenneth Clark as a splendid example of closed form, becomes totally out of place in this period except as an artificial copy.[11] The fringed cloak over the loutrophoros, datable to the third and second centuries B.C., becomes a Roman copyist's inconsistency. Neither of these assumptions seems true.

An additional observable feature of the Capitoline Aphrodite is more in keeping with the character of this time than of any other. It

was only natural that if an important and fundamentally new way of com-
prehending a space was one of the triumphs of the climax of the
Hellenistic age that one should expect to find a correspondingly
contemporaneous interpretation of the surfaces of solids. The Capitoline image (Pl. XXXVI) offers proof that this is true. Here can be seen
that sense of mass which Carpenter called plastic, rather than the
glyptic formal concept of all earlier Greek sculpture.[12] The surface
of this figure was modelled with a highly developed tactile sense, and
the undulations of the flesh are more specific than the planar variations of its ancestor the Medici Aphrodite (Pl. III).

It is true that until recently the Capitoline has been regarded as
a replica of a work of the fourth century B.C., but there are too many
outright errors in terms of that period to give it such a label. The
most recent study set forth an astute analysis of the modelling, and
emphasized the non-classical shape of the navel, whose lower contours
form a triangle, rather than an oval like that of the Medici Aphrodite
(Pls. III, XXXVI).[13] This biological detail can be studied as an
indication of a chronological sequence, going from a deep, rounded form
in the fourth century B.C. as seen on a bronze of the goddess in the
Metropolitan (Pl. VIII),[14] through an oval-like one by the early third
on the Medici (Pl. III).[15] In the latter half of the century it assumes
a triangular shape, with the apex pointed downward, like the navel of a
half-draped _anadyomene_ statue in the Vatican (Pl. XL).[16] After 150 B.C.
it commences to resemble a deep oval again, or a round button, evenly

recessed all round and convenient to drill, shapes which were fully established by around 120-90 B.C., the approximate dates of the famous Cyrene and Melos statues (Pls. XLIII, LII), or the Aphrodite, Pan and Eros group from Delos.[17]

Such a conclusion with respect to the date of the Capitoline Aphrodite becomes all the more acceptable when one compares her coiffure with the late third-century heads of the Aphrodite binding her sandal (Pl. XIV) and Arsinoë III (Pl. XX).[18] All three preserve the gently curling locks of hair before the ears following the same S curve. No parallel to them exists on the Medici figure (Pl. III) but they are found on other examples of the Capitoline type.[19] The hair atop the head is similar to a second century replica of the sandalbinder in Berlin (Pl. XXIII).[20] Thus the keynote for this period was set by a combination of pictorial and plastic qualities, characteristic of the Capitoline statue, rather than the features of the relief figure of Aphrodite on the Pergamon frieze.[21]

One could hardly expect the innovation of taking over earlier works and creatively reworking them to be without consequences. Two other examples were both adapted from the Cnidian and Medici types. The first once stood in the Troad in Northwestern Asia Minor. It is known from a copy in the magazine of the Museo Nazionale Romano, which bears the inscription, "From the Aphrodite in the Troad, Menophantos made it," and was important enough to have been reproduced a number of times.[22] The nude goddess stands, weight on left leg, in the pudica attitude like

the Medici, but retains an end of drapery like the Cnidia. It is of
little significance so far as the character or formal traits of Aphrodite are concerned, in which negative aspect it is matched by a figure
from Cyrene known as the "Maliciosa."[23] This is also a re-expression of
the pudica motif, and like the Capitoline Aphrodite, her coiffure
features two long tresses better than shoulder length. Unlike the fully
modelled form of the Capitoline, the "Maliciosa's" figure is slimmer,
and she is tilted forward almost as far as the late Hellenistic bronze
version of the Cnidia in New York (Pl. II).[24] A literal decline in
plastic volume and solidity must have commenced by the middle of the
second century B.C., for these figures approach that time, and their
rather uninspired schematization of pose and detail forecasts what is
to come.

The foregoing examples were distinguished as much by their Atticism
as by their originality. Before considering later works another should
be cited, which by its modelling and forthright employment of light and
shade is linked to the time of the Pergamon friezes. Such a work as the
so-called Aphrodite Undressing, in the Louvre (Pl. XXXVII) from its
relatively flamboyant treatment of drapery and skin recalls the Capitoline statue.[25] Because the torso is cradled against its background of
stuff, like a jewel in a case, so to speak, the effect overall is more
painterly than plastic. The work is arranged in two planes, a simple
foreground and background scheme, which, it has been pointed out above,
is indicative of the first half of the second century B.C. The opinion

may here be hazarded that this kind of figure forms an Egyptian counter-
part to the baroque, Pergamene style, and illustrates the essential
unity of Hellenistic culture at this period. It is clear that just as
the Aphrodite ideal of the third century before Christ, as seen in the
crouching (Pls. IX, X, XIII) or sandalbinding types (Pls. XIV, XV) is
more mortal and less divine than fifth and even fourth-century concepts,
the artists of figures like the Capitoline or Louvre examples (Pls.
XXXVI, XXXVII) are more interested in paying an admiring tribute to a
sensuous ideal of womanhood than to an intellectual one. It was the
pictorial, experimental, and feminine qualities of these works which
were to attract at the beginning of the next phase.

Finally, it appears that the more conservative minded at this time,
who did not accept the voluptuous vitality of the Capitoline Aphrodite
and related figures, commissioned other types which were like it only in
that they too were creative adaptations of earlier prototypes. The
statue known as the "Townley Venus" now in the British Museum, is a case
in point.[26] It appears at a glance to reproduce the Aphrodite of Arles
(Pl. I), but the combination of reversing the composition and of breaking up its overall swing by reworking the drapery to give it a many-
faceted, more independent life have removed it clearly from the sphere
of the fourth century B.C. Stylistically its closest parallels are
found in Pergamene work of around 180 B.C. which were also made as
massive visually as possible by a like handling of stuffs.[27] Like the
preceding examples discussed, the Townley statue reveals not only a

consciousness of the Attic past, but also a desire to experiment with older types, lavishing upon their reworked surfaces a new attention to detail and producing a depth of modelling in light and shade which fragmentizes the single undulating curve of the Arles prototype into accented segments.

## 2. Beginning of the End

Technical facility, smoothness of finish, and weakness of concept distinguish a sequence of statues of Aphrodite commencing around 150 B.C. No new types after that date can be attributed to Pergamon. Instead, the lesser centers such as Rhodes now begin to assume prominence. In contrast to the creative reelaborations of the first half of the second century B.C., the second phase seems to have produced decorative adaptations, indicative of an impoverishment of artistic vitality. An increase in two-dimensionality is noticeable in these sculptures.

A number of figures may be grouped under the label, the Aphrodite pudica of Rhodes, after a statue which may have been a cult image in a temple on that island.[28] The standard pose, right hand across the bust, left to the center of the hips, familiar through its revival in the Capitoline and related statues of the earlier second century B.C., is combined with the conventional half-draped arrangement known in monumental sculpture ever since the Aphrodite of Arles in the mid-fourth century (Pl. I). The new position of the costume, however, is exceedingly unconventional, for it comes only to the midpoint of the thighs,

leaving the hips entirely bared, to be held up in front by a knot of the
Isis type and by the left hand, now clutching the upper edges of the
material. The sfumato finish is excessively vague and hazy. The head,
in most of those examples in which it has survived, attracts attention
only because of the weakness of its modelling, and small size, in marked
inconsistency with the rest of the figure. This effect is heightened by
its abrupt turn to the left, so that the vertical axis is broken at the
top rather than being twisted. In this respect it is similar to the
Aphrodite binding her sandal from the Sabouroff collection, now in
Berlin, datable also to the mid-second century B.C. (Pl. XXIII).[29]
Nothing about this type of Aphrodite pudica indicates that it may ante-
date c. 150 B.C., although at one time the fourth century B.C. or, more
recently, the third have both been suggested.[30] The similarity to the
half-draped anadyomene's costume, in which a knot supports the drapery
(Pl. XL) speaks for a later date, for this kind of borrowing of isolated
motifs is typical of the second century before Christ.

It is apparent that the kind of pose struck by the Aphrodite pudica
of Rhodes gained some popularity, since there are thirty-odd surviving
examples.[31] By lowering the drapery to below the hips, and by the
device of the clutching hand, any sense of the divine presence is almost
totally lost. Yet other versions are saved from mediocrity or vulgarity
by their excellent technical execution. In this group must be included
the Aphrodite of Syracuse from Taormina, whose sensuous modelling is of
a high order.[32] Regrettably incomplete, it exists only from the waist

down. Although it is a Roman copy of the imperial period, it recalls
the almost baroque handling of flesh still in vogue about 150 B.C., to
which its original seems to have belonged, comparable to the early
second century date of the Capitoline statue's original. Among other
adaptations in which one hand goes to the hair, the other to precari-
ously supported drapery at hip level, should be counted the so-called
Aphrodite "Unguente" in the Vatican, who has been wrongly restored as
holding a perfume jar (Pl. XLII).[33] Her costume still shows traces of a
supporting hand, while the other, also restored, but correctly, raises a
lock of hair in more orthodox anadyomene fashion. Among other variations may be cited an example of the nude anadyomene, in which one hand
went to the hair, while the other held a perfume jar or mirror, as in a
statuette from Rhodes now in the Metropolitan (Pl. XLI).[34]

Once the idea of a syncretistic combination of motifs had been
established, other arrangements followed, for another known type which
appears to have originated in this period was the result of a fusion
between the crouching and anadyomene motifs. It is known in a little
statuette from Rhodes (Pl. XII, bottom) and a number of replicas from
Egypt.[35] This sequence probably commenced about 125 B.C. and continued
into the first century B.C. and after. Such a figure illustrates that
the borrowing to which this period was addicted extended beyond the
reuse of motifs and devices of an earlier age. Its finish, a deceptively skinlike sfumato of exceptionally exaggerated softness, recalls
a post-Praxitelean technique seen on the head of a girl from Chios in

Boston of c. 300 B.C.[36] And its thinness from front to back substan-
tiates a conclusion that, as an interest in pictorial illusionism, seen
here in the modelling, increased, a desire to give works of sculpture a
genuine three-dimensional existence declined. Similarly flattened is a
bronze example of the Aphrodite anadyomene from Courtrai (Pl. XLV),
recently dated to the second half of the second century B.C., but which
could almost as easily belong with the Providence bronze (Pls. VI, VIX)
and a number of others like the Venus of Grenoble made about the time of
Christ.[37] These all display a type of modelling in which the flattened
forms are accompanied by a subtle elongation of proportion. As a
Hellenistic device to introduce an artificial elegance into the composition, and used in marble works with a sfumato modelling, it appears
in an Aphrodite anadyomene with a dolphin, now in the Cairo Museum, from
Egypt (Pl. XXII, no. 27454).[38] Here, and in a similar figure from
Alexandria, though larger and with a Triton, in Dresden,[39] the two-
dimensional effect characteristic of the second half of the second
century B.C. is heightened by the subsidiary mass beside Aphrodite's
right leg.

The enduring popularity of the anadyomene motif and of the goddess
in Egypt is testified to by the upper half of a statue of this type from
Horbeit, now in the Louvre (Pl. XXXV).[40] The lower portion was probably
covered with drapery. The indifferent quality speaks for a chronological attribution to the late Hellenistic period. A mould of the nude
anadyomene (Pl. XLVII) from the same country and in the Cairo Museum

proves that as the divine significance of Aphrodite decreased, her popularity did not wane.[41] Yet the decline in original production at major Hellenistic centers of sculpture did not affect the quality of work in some of the smaller corners of the Eastern Mediterranean. Among the finest known examples of the Aphrodite anadyomene must be placed the example from Cyrenaica, found near Benghazi, and today on loan to the University Museum in Philadelphia (Pl. XLVIII).[42] Its smooth cut below the hips may have meant that it was designed to be placed on a surface made to represent water. At any rate, it is so finely carved it appears translucent where the stone is thin, and thus a sfumato effect is achieved without literal imitation of skin. Only the stiffness of the rather mechanically straight hair-tresses held in each hand prevent this marble from being a genuine masterpiece. It indicates that the bizarre combinations of the mid-second century B.C. were succeeded by a sober imitativeness.

### 3. The Advent of Neo-Classicism

At the very end of this period, and extending into the last century before Christ, there appear works of plastic art characterized by a very real attempt to capture the spirit of an earlier age. Since the examples of Aphrodite anadyomene just discussed have been adaptations rather than imitations, it should prove profitable to continue an examination of this type.

The most outstanding representation of Aphrodite rising from the sea is the full-size marble found at Cyrene and now at the Terme in Rome

(Pls. XLIII, XLIV).[43]  Various attempts have been made to date this
statue to the early second century B.C.[44] or to label it a copy, made
during the late Roman imperial period, of a bronze original of the third
quarter of the third century before Christ.[45]  It would indeed seem
unreasonable to define it as an original conception, and whether it
harks back to an earlier bronze is a matter for subjective evaluation,
but a detailed inspection of the modelling and comparative evidence
makes the first century B.C. a highly plausible date.  The pose is relatively straight and stiff, so the figure stands erect.  Yet the problem
of weight and support is not dealt with clearly.  From the front, the
weight of the body is divided unevenly, while from the back it obviously
falls upon the right leg (Pls. XLIII, XLIV).  The effect of standing
stiffly is due to the elongated dimensions of the legs, for both shin
and thigh are out of proportion even to the abnormally long-waisted
torso above.  Yet such an inconsistency is forgotten when one regards
the marble from a rear view, unless one finds the thinness of the legs
disturbing.  The total visual effect is remarkably like the bronze
Aphrodite in Providence (Pls. VI, VII), which also belongs to the final
phases of Hellenism, perhaps even to the Augustan age.[46]  The unifying
tendency of the smoothly finished, almost slick surface can not overcome
these inconsistencies.

A further lack of harmony may be perceived in the modelling.  From
a frontal point there appears to be an unarticulated fatness to the
thighs, and the handling of the kneecap is rather schematized, although

both features, given the right living model, can be classified as highly
naturalistic. The torso itself is exceptionally closely modelled from
the front, but not at the back. Glancing briefly at the anadyomene
statuette from the vicinity of Benghazi (Pl. XLVIII), whose assumed date
was placed above at not long after 150 B.C., one sees another marble,
distinguished from the Cyrene example yet coming from the same political
and cultural unit. Compared to the little figure, the larger one
possesses an abnormally thin thorax, and a shallow circular dot of a
navel rather than a near triangle. Below the line of the backbone and
above the crease of the buttocks, the Benghazi anadyomene's lower back
ends in an inverted triangle, whose upper points are defined by two
small depressions in the skin, and from there lightly indented lines run
to the apex of the triangle headed downward, at the meeting line of the
buttocks. A similar anatomical construction appears on the back of the
Aphrodite in a group from Delos, while the grooved lines, but not the
circular indentations, are modelled on the skin of the goddess from
Melos.[47] One should note too that the outline of her navel is identical
to that of the Cyrene figure. Now the conventional and logical date for
the Delos group is c. 100 B.C., on epigraphical grounds. It may also be
pointed out that an Apollo citharoedos from Cyrene attributed to Timarchides has been dated to the same decades.[48] The baroque swing to its
torso and drapery is, however, a far cry from the stiff, precise dryness
of the Aphrodite excavated at the same city. It may therefore be concluded that the goddess from Cyrene belongs later in that circle known
as classicistic in the first century B.C.

The foregoing conclusion can be strengthened by reference to several examples of the half-draped Aphrodite anadyomene. First the replica from Alba Fucens may be cited (Pl. LI).[49] This figure's torso is inclined forward in the manner of other late Hellenistic Aphrodites, like the bronze replica of Cnidia in the Metropolitan (Pl. II),[50] and its right arm was flung awkwardly up and out in a position similar to that of the half-clad Cyrene Apollo. The central part of the body rests on a draped lower portion, whose covering folds of material create deep shadows, and, with tremendous variety but little sense of consistency, form an unstable visual base. From front to back, the marble slab is cut quite thin, making for a rather narrow profile view. The triangular shape of the navel recalls the presumed third century B.C. date of this type.[51] This statue, dated to 100 B.C. by its excavators, can hardly furnish support for placing the Aphrodite of Cyrene at the same time.

A second example reveals that it was unlikely that the famous goddess in the Terme belonged to the imperial age. At Sinuessa in South Italy there was discovered a partly-clad Aphrodite anadyomene, now in the Museo Nazionale at Naples (Pl. L, bottom).[52] Life-size and of local stone with no sfumato finish, the statue is nude from the thighs up. A typical Roman recreation of a Hellenistic type as produced from the first century B.C. on, it bears some similarities in the modelling of its fleshy hips, round drilled navel, narrow waist, and raised left arm and shoulder, rather than the right, to the Aphrodite of Cyrene. As a mirror image of the usual pose and arrangement, the Cyrene figure, with

its shoulders and stance reversed, and dolphin at the statue's right, is
characteristic of the period just before the advent of exact copying
techniques, but figures made in this way were occasionally copied themselves. If one looks again from the Cyrene example (Pl. XLIII) to the
Sinuessa piece (Pl. L, bottom), certain differences in the direction of
more naturalistic and less abstract modelling show themselves. The
contrasts are most evident in the handling of the soft flesh under the
navel and its band of supporting muscle below, and in the relative firmness of the breasts. A profile photograph of the Sinuessa statue
reveals more of a naturalistically indicated sense of weight, compared
to the more geometric cones of the Cyrene marble. Finally, the abundant
crinkles of the Sinuessa's drapery may be matched against the character
of the folds of the garment over the dolphin's tail in the other work as
evidence of the Roman date of the former and in support of a date before
the time of Christ for the latter. Thus the Aphrodite of Cyrene may be
bracketed by the statues of the same goddess from Alba Fucens and from
Sinuessa to validate its attribution to the first century B.C. as a
classicistic monument. Still decidedly Greek, it must be located in the
early decades of that period.

The renowned marble from Cyrene has been associated with Rhodian
work of that period, but the quality of its finish, a sfumato typical of
Rhodes in the late second and first centuries B.C., can hardly have been
limited to that area alone.[53] On the other hand, its elongation and
stiffness of form beneath the dry smoothness of its modelling must have

been preceded by an incipient schematization of surface which fore-
shadowed the classicism, or, if one prefers, the neo-classicism, of the
first century B.C., before the Laokoon's rhetorical revival of the
pathos of high Hellenistic, if indeed, that work belongs around 50
B.C.[54] Along with an increasing hardness of form must have gone the
last stages of the free eclecticism discussed above as characterizing
the middle and third quarter of the second century B.C. The point at
which a regular codification of form and type alike commenced has been
placed around 130 B.C.[55] One example from the end of the last third of
this century may suffice to illustrate the change. It is an Aphrodite
in the Fogg Museum of Art in Cambridge (Pl. XXXVIII).[56] It is partly
draped in a manner which bares the torso in front, but covers the back
and the lower limbs. The rather mechanical and evenly spaced ridges of
the material are interspersed along the outside of the legs with folds
arranged like a "V" on its side. The front view reveals an ample,
modelled abdomen whose broadness contrasts slightly with the more
maidenlike proportions above. It may be compared with another, partly
sitting, partly leaning, on a rock, whose pose and similar costume agree
closely with the Dirce of the Farnese Bull Group, also a Rhodian work
(Pliny, N.H. 36.33-34), as has been observed.[57] Each of these female
figures reveals a calmer handling of form and costume, unlike the
examples of the previous period. They also display such a loss of
originality that they, except for Dirce, may represent nymphs, for there
is actually nothing to distinguish them as Aphrodite.[58] Nevertheless,
it was from this kind of work that a repertoire of types was drawn

during the Roman period, as a comparable work of doubtful identity in Worcester proves (Pl. XXXIX).[59] The execution of this marble is not very exciting, and the drapery is more conventional than in the Fogg Museum statue. The fact that it is impossible to tell whether either was intended to be an Aphrodite reveals a decline in the ideal of the goddess, and indeed of the very concept of type, which had been at the basis of so much Greek art for over half a millenium. The group from Delos, in which Aphrodite, aided by Eros, repulses Pan, commissioned by a Syrian merchant, or other groups in which she threatens Eros with a slipper or a wreath known as a _cestus_, also reveal the change, compared to her earlier, more dignified appearances in sculpture.[60]

It was inevitable that the classical type of Aphrodite should be revived too, given the eclectic spirit of the time and its increasing respect for the art of the past. Such an urge led to the creation of one of the last plastic expressions of the goddess within the Hellenistic orbit, the Aphrodite of Melos (Pl. LII).[61] Behind it lay the early stages of the revival discussed above, stimulated by the patronage of the Romans who were flocking to Rhodes, Delos and other commercial centers. At Delos, for example, they established their own _agora_, and in niches along the wall placed portraits of themselves, whose specific heads are in odd contrast to the nude idealized bodies of athletic Polykleitan types on which they were placed.[62] The artists who worked in these trading towns came from Attica, or were inspired by the revival of Attic style which had begun there as early as the mid-second century B.C.[63] The sculptor of the Aphrodite of Melos was [Ages-or Alex-] andros, son of Henidos and came originally from Antioch on the Meander, Phrygia, according to an inscription on a plinth, now lost, found with the statue in a niche or small exedra. Cut into this base was a square hole, and a pillar upon which the left arm once rested is usually included in hypothetical restorations. Since head, torso, a few fragments and draped lower portion alone survive, it is impossible to reconstruct the original pose. The type, however, is quite evidently an attempt to recapture the essence of the figure known as the Aphrodite of Capua, whose original was at Corinth.[64] Both the works from Capua and from Melos have drapery ascending from left to right across the hips and a raised leg on the observer's right. The torsos are nude; both are twisted, and the heads exude an air of placid reserve. Details, like the hair parted in the center, and a deeply cut oval navel, can be found on both, although the Capua Aphrodite wears a _sphendone_ above the roll of hair at the front and sides of her head, some short strands of hair on the nape of the neck have escaped from the chignon of the Melos figure and the latter's proportions are more matronly. Both conceptions of the goddess are indebted to works of the fifth century B.C., like the draped Pheidian Aphrodite with her left foot on a tortoise.[65]

Beyond these resemblances, differences prevail. The unified harmony of the Capua goddess, to be restored as writing on a shield, is due to her own concentration and lack of concern for any spectator, and a single consistent, internal rhythm from bottom to top, with no perceptibly emphasized visual break between the draped and nude halves

of the body. The Aphrodite of Melos lacks this inner unity, and the

compositional lines of her figure radiate outwards. Her raised leg is

canted to her right, while the folds of the garment beside and above it

lead to her left. In other words, the apparent base of her composition

is an "X" whose visual lines may be contrasted to the parallelogram-

shaped base of the Capua's drapery. The center section of the statue

from Melos acts as a neutral zone, above which occurs a change in di-

rection, for the chest is turned so the upper half of the body of the

goddess faces toward her left, in opposition to the lower diagonal of

her left leg. Yet both these lines appear as diagonals, joined by the

abdomen, to the spectator. In this respect the composition recalls the

animating "S" curve of Praxiteles, but made more angular. That this was

a conscious attempt can be legitimately assumed, not only on account of

the classicistic character of the age in sculpture, but also because of

the indebtedness of the features of the head to Praxitelean prototypes.

Its dreamy yet pensive far-away look of inner reflection suggests

strongly the indistinct, hazy qualities of the Boston Bartlett head.[66]

The impression is dispelled upon close examination of the former's

crisper eyelids, lips, and hair, revealing how the expertly handled use

of a running drill mechanically reconstructed the masterworks of a

bygone age.

One should not turn away from the Aphrodite of Melos, nor from the

other examples of late Hellenistic art discussed here, mocking at man's inability to turn back in time. Judged by their own standards, the four

greater works presented above, the Capitoline, Benghazi, Cyrene, and

Melos Aphrodites all surpass the lesser ones with which they have been

included. The statue from Melos is now thought to have been made in

Delos between 120 and 90 B.C., and [Ages- or Alex-]andros to have been

trained in Attica, the stronghold of traditionalism in Greek civili-

zation.[67] Charbonneaux has made a convincing case for the same artist's

authorship of a bust of Mithridates the Great, in the Louvre, the last

champion before Cleopatra of the Hellenistic world.[68] The sculptor's

significant success in meaningfully remaking a classic image of Aphro-

dite demonstrates that Hellenistic art had come full circle.

CHAPTER VI

CONCLUSION

The foregoing studies, limited as they were to specific chronological phases of Hellenistic sculpture, and focussed on successive single
types of Aphrodite, lead to such summary statements as can be based upon
this investigation. First, what sort of character does the goddess
assume during the last century properly defined as Hellenistic, the
period between 100 B.C. and the Augustan age? Having reached a point
from which the entire field can be assessed, two further questions
suggest themselves. A number of the statues of Aphrodite previously
cited and analyzed have been labelled examples of Hellenistic rococo.
Whether this nomenclature is accurate or a misunderstanding, an open
question, deserves consideration here. Finally, justification for the
study can be found in the new light it throws upon traditional interpretations of late Greek sculpture, without going into needless recapitula-
tion of what has already been said.

1. The First Century B.C., an Epilogue

Hellenistic statues of Aphrodite produced during the last hundred
years before Christ continue but intensify the traditions and innovations of the previous century. The Aphrodite from Cyrene (Pls. XLIII,
XLIV) may or may not be a Rhodian work, but its surface treatment and

relative frontality are akin to the work of that region early in the
first century.[1] It was there that the final echoes of "Asian baroque,"
if the style of Pergamon may be so described, could be found.[2] Nearby,
in Caria, the archaistic Aphrodite of Aphrodisias (cf. Pl. XXV, bottom)
reveals that a second strain at the time was a deliberate archaism,
which continued unabated into the Roman era.[3] On her skirt are depicted
the Three Graces, who also assume plastic form at Cyrene.[4] Their appearance follows a prior recording in painting, which may date back as far
as the third century B.C.[5] Priority exists in another medium also for
the so-called epigrammatic Aphrodite, Pan, and Eros group from Delos,
now in Athens.[6] The aggressiveness of Pan and the response of the goddess, armed with a slipper, echo literary mention of her inability to
chastise mythological figures who interfere mischievously with human
love. The goddess in this group, whose banal character shows how much
of the traditional force and dignity of Aphrodite as a conception had
vanished by this date, imitates, except for the hand holding the slipper,
the standard _pudica_ type, although she stands with the weight on her
right, away from Pan. Beside the secularization seen in the "pantoufle"
group must be placed the more dignified recasting of older versions
exemplified by the Aphrodite of Melos (Pl. LII), a figure which may have
been accompanied by Eros when complete.[7]

The spectrum of artistic features and plastic expressions covered
by these examples proves that baroque, pictorial, archaistic, literary
and academic tendencies were all present to some degree in the

Hellenistic sculpture of the first century B.C. The lack of predomi-
nance of any single trait left the way open for a further loss of
continuity, but the old traditions were revived deliberately in various
poorly proportioned works. An example, whose likely identity is Aphrodite, is a transparently-clothed female figure in Athens with a loop of
drapery across the upper legs.[8] It is artificially long waisted, however, and fails to recapture the unified rhythmic sweep which energized
the monuments of the fifth or fourth centuries B.C.

The mixed tendencies present during the earlier half of the first
century before Christ, one can claim, were fused in the Laocoon.[9] Yet
even if that work belongs to c. 150 B.C. rather than 50 B.C., it is
clear that the focus of Greek art was turning toward the preservation
and transmission of its heritage by the use of various copying devices,
as well as by the free copies which had been made ever since c. 200 B.C.,
if not earlier. There is no question about the popularity of Greek
types, and with them, of Aphrodite, in the Roman epoch. The figure of
her acquired recently by the Metropolitan and the famous Medici Aphrodite (Pl. III) are both products of this time.[10]

After 50 B.C. it probably is equally proper to refer to the goddess
as Venus. Caesar popularized her cult, commissioning Arcesileos to
create a Venus Genetrix, so wrote Pliny (N.H. 35.156), as the divine
founder of his house.[11] The tradition was strengthened by his successor
Octavian when the latter had Apelles' painting of Aphrodite anadyomene
shipped to Rome and installed there (Pliny, N.H. 35.91). As Greece

became Roman, so Aphrodite became Venus. That enigmatic type known as the Esquiline Venus, if it should be proven to be a Roman pastiche, would only make clearer what is already known, that the late Hellenistic habit of recombining the types and motifs of the past lived on.[12] So too did the tradition of copying, thanks to which it is possible in part to reconstruct the history of Hellenistic art.

### 2. Was there a Hellenistic Rococo?

This study has attempted to define the major plastic types of Aphrodite evolved during the Hellenistic period. Several of these, for example, the Rhodian version of the crouching Aphrodite and the statues of her binding her sandal, can be labelled rococo in spirit. Rococo, historically, is a name given to the continental art of Western Europe in the eighteenth century before the advent of neo-classicism and after the baroque age of the seventeenth. Rococo as a label has come to mean a lightness of motive, and a mood of gaiety, somewhat irresponsible, expressed in works of no monumental significance, distinguished by technical facility, and, usually, smallness of scale. Hence it implies a mood, delight for its own sake, and is distinct from folk art through its sophistication. Rococo is only possible at the end of a period of development when the prerequisites of artistic expression in a given style have been mastered and experimentation in a minor key with the accepted modes appears desirable and is possible.[13]

The attempt to label later Hellenistic sculpture rococo has pro-duced a cliché which undoubtedly made much of its art more appealing to the modern mind.[14] Its more human aspects, and perhaps the decorative ones, became comprehensible and likeable at first sight, like genre art. They also became about as significant in terms of content.

By distorting the more unprejudiced views of Hellenistic sculpture it is clear that the benefits of calling some of its products rococo have not been an unmitigated gain. To name two well-known masterpieces, both supine sleeping figures of c. 200 B.C. which discredit the application of the term -- reference can be made to the Barberini Faun in Munich and the sleeping Eros type, both apparently originals.[15] Do the former's heavy accents, serious naturalism and large scale, contrasted to the childlike charm and smaller though life-size scale of the latter, mean that the Faun is baroque, and the Eros rococo? It is a logical distinction, yet if rococo means a style which succeeded another in time with clarity, even accompanied by some overlapping, does not such a conjunction throw doubts upon the thesis?

The Aphrodite who binds her sandal fulfills all the definitions of a rococo piece but one -- it is too early, for it was developed in the last quarter of the third century B.C.[16] Its predecessor, the crouching Aphrodite, is likewise too early, and the subsequent versions are not all the same type (Pl. XII, bottom).[17] Can the Benghazi example of the anadyomene (Pl. XLVIII) fit the label rococo?[18] On the basis of its scale, an affirmative answer is possible, and the sculptor attempted clearly to charm, but he succeeded in making a highly dignified figurine,

and the original conception leads through figures like the one from
Horbeit, now in the Louvre (Pl. XXXV), back again to the third century.[19]

Thus most of the examples of Aphrodite at least that one can call
rococo are second century B.C. versions of originals of an earlier date.
It was demonstrated in the previous chapter that the multi-faceted
second century was an eclectic one; although it exhibited surpassing
skill in art, its creativeness does not quite coincide with rococo as
the term is commonly employed. It is easy to emphasize the popularity
of smaller works of art, but these appear to have commenced with subjects like the sandalbinder, the bronze dancer from Alexandria, or the
satyr looking at his tail, in the middle of the Hellenistic period and
before the second century B.C.[20] All have that kind of charm called
genre and are originals of the period. The second century is not
rococo; perhaps it might have been if the Attalids had not chosen to
emulate classic Athens, and thus wilfully turned the current of Hellenistic sculpture into a sudden awareness of the greatness of the past.
And the closest approach to rococo in later Greek sculpture precedes
the baroque of Pergamon in the first half of the second century before
Christ.

### 3. Reevaluations of Hellenistic Sculpture

The assessment of one aspect of the material covered in this thesis
leads to a consideration of it as a whole. Through an examination of
different types of Aphrodite evolved in the course of the Hellenistic
age, light has been thrown upon her changing character as well as that

of the era. The steady development of nude or half-draped varieties was quite obviously indebted to the innovations of Praxiteles in the second half of the fourth century B.C. His immediate followers in sculpture produced types which became almost equally renowned, and the contemporary painter Apelles, whose picture of Aphrodite, among other works, brought him fame, initiated painted depictions which inspired plastic versions before the end of the third century B.C. Around 250 B.C., Doidalsas of Bithynia produced the crouching type, whose three-dimensionality records a distinct advance in the Hellenistic sculptor's art. This was followed by the half-draped and nude versions of the Aphrodite anadyomene, and the sandalbinder, of the last quarter of the third century before Christ, completes a sequence. Artistically, their increasing naturalism establishes a logical development linking the third to the fourth centuries B.C. without interruptions. Through them can be seen the increasing humanization of the gods of Greece, as each of these anthropomorphic images is less divine and more of a genre figure than the last. The second century statues are different in character, for here the frankly refashioned older types testify to a renewed self-consciousness with respect to earlier tradition. After a phase of eclecticism, Hellenistic art refounds itself in the first century B.C. on a neo-classic base under Roman patronage as the ancient world passes under Roman leadership. The comparative pictorial richness and unifaciality of several examples of Aphrodite from Egypt (Pl. XXXVII) and Asia Minor reveal how features associated with Roman art commenced within the orbit of late Hellenistic.[21] Painting, in relation to sculpture, often considered important

only after 100 B.C., actually began to be of increasing significance
long before; it underlay the appearance in sculpture of the anadyomene
in the third century B.C., and a more complete record would show a
growing attention to naturalistic details, space concepts and drama,
paralleling and influencing its sister art. In sculpture, at any rate,
the Hellenistic period should not be differentiated too sharply from the
preceding Greek epochs until 200 B.C. In it, the evolution of the female
nude occupies the same position that the male kouros did in archaic and
classical art, as an index of understanding of the human figure. The
unsuspected richness of inventive designs traceable to the second half
of the third century B.C. is comparable to a similar manifestation in
ripe archaic at the end of the sixth.

Of the various aspects which this study has indicated should be
viewed in a different light, two are worthy of further mention. First,
the continuity of development which has been demonstrated is also geographical. The artistic tradition of Ionia, associated with that of
mainland Greece in the sixth and fifth centuries B.C. through the
presence of Ionian artists in Attica, was reinforced during the fourth
by journeys of artists like Praxiteles from Greece to Western Asia
Minor, and commissions at Knidos, Cos, Halicarnasseus and elsewhere.
Ionia, once a colonial relation, became the wealthier relative by the
third century B.C., which was of inestimable importance for the primary
development of the Hellenistic tradition there.

Second, the importance of the various cities and artistic centers
in Asia Minor and along its coast raises the question of the relative
significance of Alexandria.  The popularity of various Hellenistic types
which were not initiated in Egypt but whose vogue was widespread there,
such as the anadyomene or the sandalbinder (Pl. XXII, nos. 27454,
27456),[22] shows at once the strength and weakness of Greek culture in a
non-Greek land.  Alexandria was the first and, until the rise of Rome,
the foremost of the great cosmopolitan cities of antiquity.  The Ptolemaic patronage of learning and the arts was sophisticated but not
especially creative.  Politically, their biggest job was to popularize
Greek standards.  For this task, figures like Aphrodite were eminently
fitted.  Their popularity there is quite significant as an index to one
of the means of strengthening unity by means of symbols with universal
appeal.

Thus light has been shed upon the question of Hellenistic schools
as well.  By assembling examples with a varied provenience, insight has
been gained into the problem of the degree to which Hellenistic art was
local in inspiration and the extent to which it was international.[23]
The ease and rapidity with which types of Aphrodite were diffused illustrate how much homogeneity underlay the apparent and real diversity of
the Hellenistic cities and kingdoms.  Just as the creation of originals
in Asia Minor strengthens an understanding of the continuity of the
Greek tradition there, so also does the wide distribution of the various
replicas reinforce our understanding of the basic unity of Hellenistic
civilization.

Finally it should be emphasized that this investigation has been an effort to combine the principles of archaeology and the history of art, for archaeological evidence has been employed to buttress conclusions drawn from an iconographic study of changes in the form and motifs expressed by the varieties of different types. It has been based upon the conviction that as much attention should be paid to the capacity of the various replicas to mirror their own time as is customarily given to them as evidence for recreating the first conception. It is important to realize that they provide an index to changing standards in design and taste, and can throw light upon the character of periods subsequent to their primary creation. By a discriminating analysis of examples of a single Hellenistic type, this kind of a study can show the degrees of innovation, tradition, and imitation in that society through whose efforts much of the Greek tradition was passed on to Rome and the Western world. Amid the changing esteem in which Hellenistic sculpture has been held, it is hoped that the foregoing discussions have avoided equally extremes of adulation or of aspersion in charting changing plastic ideals of Aphrodite.

NOTES TO CHAPTER I

1. M. Bieber, Sculpture of the Hellenistic Age (New York, 1955) 6;
   G. Richter, "Who Made the Roman Portrait Statues -- Greeks or
   Romans?" ProcPhilSoc 95, 2 (1951) 189-208; J. Toynbee, The
   Hadrianic School: A Chapter in the History of Greek Art (Cambridge
   1934) xi-xxii.

2. M. Bieber loc. cit.

3. C. Bell, Art (London 1914) 23.

4. OCD, s.v. "Sculpture, Greek," pt. 10.

5. K. Clark. The Nude: A Study in Ideal Form (New York 1956) 89.

6. Ibid. 350.

7. P. Carpenter, ArtB 39 (1957) 67-73.

8. Ibid. 67-68.

9. (New York 1951) 27-33.

10. See also D. Thimme, "The Masters of the Pergamon Gigantomachy,"
    AJA 50 (1946) 352.

11. Op. cit. 68.

12. Vom antiken Rokoko (Vienna 1921).

13. G. Krahmer, in "Stilphasen der hellenistischen Plastik," RM 38-39
    (1923-24) 138-89; "Eine Ehrung für Mithridates VI Eupator in
    Pergamon," GottNachr., Philcl.-Hist. Klasse (1927) 53-91; and
    "Hellenisztikus Lenny-Szobrecska Budapesten," ArchErt 41 (1927)

1-30. Later studies based on Krahmer; R. Horn, "Stehende weibliche Gewandstatuen in der hellenistischen Plastik," RM Ergänzungsheft 2 (1931); V. Muller, "A Chronology of Greek Sculpture, 400-40 B.C.," ArtB 20 (1938) 359-418; L. Laurenzi, "Lineamenti di arte ellenistica," Arti Figurative: Rivista d'arte antica e moderna 1 (1945) 12-28.

14. Op. cit. 68.

15. G. Krahmer, RM 38-39 (1923-24) 154, especially his analysis of the girl from Anzio, whose composition possesses open and closed elements.

16. Infra, Ch. II, 50-51.

17. M. Bieber op. cit. 40, Fig. 102. on the Tyche, and 66-67, Figs. 214-29, on Demosthenes.

18. Ibid. 40, Figs. 97-100; R. Carpenter, "Observations on Familiar Statuary in Rome," MAAR 18 (1941) 70-73, Pl. 23; S. Aurigemma, The Baths of Diocletian and Museo Nazionale Romano (Rome 1947) 35, no. 50170, Pls. 32, 33.

19. M. Bieber op. cit. (supra, n. 1) 78-79, Figs. 272-77.

20. Cf. especially the marble head of Berenice II, in Benghazi, illustrated in M. Bieber op. cit. 92, Figs. 346-47.

21. M. Bieber op. cit. 110-11, Figs. 438-45.

22. R. Carpenter, ArtB 39 (1957) 71.

23. Aphrodite of Melos, J. Charbonneaux, "La Vénus de Milo et Mithridate le Grand," La Revue des Arts 1 (1951) 8-16, Figs. 1-14; Delos group, M. Bulard, "Aphrodite, Pan et Éros," BCH 30 (1906) 610-31,

Pls. 13-15, and G. Krahmer, RM 38-39 (1923-24) 183 and n. 5; Aphrodite of Cyrene, S. Aurigemma op. cit. 38, no. 72115, Pl. 39, and G. Gullini, "Su alcune sculture del tardo Ellenismo," Arti Figurative 3 (1947) 67-70.

24. M. Bieber op. cit. 39-42, Figs. 94-111.

25. L. Caskey, Museum of Fine Arts, Boston: Catalogue of Greek and Roman Sculpture (Cambridge [Mass.] 1925) 118-20, no. 56 and 122-23, no. 58. The bronze is identified only tentatively as Arsinoe II, but it is difficult to label as Arsinoe III, on the basis of existing portraits of that queen.

26. R. Carpenter loc. cit.

27. M. Bieber op. cit. 164, Figs. 698-99.

28. R. Carpenter op. cit. 71-72; G. Krahmer, RM 38-39, (1923-24) 139-42, 170-73; M. Bieber op. cit. 113-18, Figs. 458-70.

29. A. Furtwängler and P. Wolters, Beschreibung der Glyptothek zu München (2d. ed. 1910) no. 218; M. Hirmer and R. Lullies, Greek Sculpture (New York 1957) 75, Pls. 234-35; G. Richter, Metropolitan Museum of Art: Handbook of the Greek Collection (Cambridge [Mass.] 1953) 123-24, Pl. 102, 103b.

30. M. Bieber op. cit. 109-10, Figs. 430-36, and 110, n. 29.

31. H. Hoffman, "Foreign Influence and Native Invention in Archaic Greek Altars," AJA 57 (1953) 189-95, Pls. 55-60 and ns. 62, 64, p. 195.

32. R. Carpenter op. cit. 72; ibid. MAAR 18 (1941) 73-81.

33. R. Horn op. cit. (supra n. 13) 49-51.

34. M. Hirmer and R. Lullies op. cit. 24-25, 74-75, Pls. 232-33.

35. M. Bieber op. cit. (supra, n. 1) 118 and n. 62, Figs. 471-72, does
    not interpret the period in this manner, writing of the Zeus from
    the temple of Hera at Pergamon, "Ippel (AM 37, 1912, 261, 316 ff.,
    Figs. 11-15, Pls. 22a and 26) and Horn (RM Ergänzungsheft 2, 1931,
    49ff., Pl. 20, no. 2) see a relaxation of intensity and evidence of
    academic traits in this statue, a view which I can not share."
    But see also her explanation of late Hellenistic classicism, pp.
    156-59.

36. V. Muller loc. cit. (supra, n. 13).

37. A. Giuliano, "La Afrodite Callipige di Siracusa," Arch Cl 5 (1953)
    210-14, Pls. 100-103.

38. E. Schmidt, "Ueber einige Fälle der Uebertragung gemalter Figuren
    in Rundplastik," Festschrift für Paul Arndt (Munich 1925) 96-114;
    R. Lullies, "Zur Drei-Grazien-Gruppe," MdI 1 (1948) 45-52; M.
    Bieber op. cit. 147-50 and n. 87, p. 147.

39. T. Homolle, "Statue de Caius Ofellius: sur une oeuvre signée des
    artistes Dionysios et Polycles, BCH 5 (1881) 390-96, Pl. 12, and
    "Les Romains a Délos, BCH 8 (1884) 115; E. Lapalus, L'Agora des
    Italiens ("L'Exploration archéologique de Délos 19: L'École franc.
    d'Athènes," Paris 1939) 41-60; A. Lawrence, Later Greek Sculpture:
    Its Influence on East and West (London 1927) 34, Pls. 57, 58a. The
    Roman practice of placing portrait heads on the bodies of known
    statue types of Greek gods is actually a continuation of this
    Hellenistic custom. Although the Greeks did not generally indulge

themselves in this way, by extension the tradition may be said to
have begun with the representations of Alexander the Great. Cf. G.
Richter, ProcPhilSoc 95, 2 (1951) 191-208; M. Bieber, "The Portraits of Alexander the Great," ibid. 93, 5 (1949) 274-427.

40. R. Carpenter, "Apollonios Nestoros," MAAR 6 (1927) 133-36, Pls. 49-
51, made the identification of the boxer, and MAAR 18 (1941) 81-83,
Pl. 25, has advocated a first century B.C. date for the Hellenistic
ruler; G. Richter, in Three Critical Periods in Greek Sculpture
(New York 1951) 67-70, would place all three in the mid-second
century B.C. On the ruler and the boxer together, see: P.
Williams, "Amykos and the Discuri," AJA 49 (1945) 330-47, Figs.
1-11, with Carpenter's response, "The Identity of the Ruler," ibid.
353-57, Figs. 1-3. One of the best replicas of the Homer is in
Boston, see: L. Caskey op. cit. (supra, n. 25) 115-17, n. 55; cf.
R. Boehringer and E. Boehringer, Homer, Bildnisse und Nachweise
(Breslau 1939).

41. On the worship of Aphrodite in ancient religion, see: Ency. Brit.
s. v. "Aphrodite"; L. Farrell, The Cults of the Greek States
(Oxford 1896) II, 618-69; W. Guthrie, The Greeks and their Gods
(London 1950) 30, 101; M. Nilsson, Geschichte der griechischen
Religion II: Die hellenistische und römische Zeit ("Handbuch der
Altertumswissenschaft" V, II, 2; Munich 1950) 277-94, same as his
"Problems of the History of Greek Religion in the Hellenistic and
Roman Age," HThR 36 (1943) 251-76; A. Nock, Magical Notes, JEA 11
(1925) 154-58; ibid. "Religious Attitudes of the Ancient Greeks,"

ProcPhilSoc 85 (1942) 472-85; OCD, s. v. "Aphrodite," and "Aphrodite in Art"; RE, including article in Supplement I (1932), s. v. "Aphrodite"; L. Preller and C. Robert, Griechische Mythologie (5th ed. Berlin 1894) I, 345-85; P. Roscher ed., Ausf. Lex. der gr. u. röm. Mythologie, s. v. "Aphrodite." On the representation of Aphrodite in ancient religion and art, see: L. Bernoulli, Aphrodite: ein Baustein zur griechischen Kunstmythologie (Leipzig 1873); H. Goetz, "Aphrodite Urania: an Asiatic Cult in Ancient Greece, and a Corinthian Bronze in the Baroda Museum," Bulletin of the Baroda State Museum and Picture Gallery 3, 2 (1946) 1-15, Figs. 1-7.

42. G. Blümel, Staatliche Museen zu Berlin, Katalog der Sammlung antiker Skulpturen III: Katalog der griechischen Skulpturen des fünften und vierten Jahrhunderts vor Christus (Berlin 1929) 5, K. 5, Pls. 6-7; E. Langlotz, Phidiasprobleme (Frankfurt am Main 1947) 83, Pl. 26; C. Picard, Manuel d'archéologie grecque, la sculpture II: Période classique - Ve. siècle (1 vol. in 2 pts. Paris 1939) pt. 1, 342-44, Fig. 146; H. Schrader, Pheidias (Frankfurt am Main 1924) 73-74, Fig. 57, 266, Fig. 243.

43. H. Süsserott, Griechische Plastik des vierten Jahrhunderts vor Christus: Untersuchungen zur Zeitbestimmung (Frankfurt am Main 1938) 141-80, Pls. 20, 2; 32, 1, 3; 33, 3; 36, 1.

44. M. Nilsson, Greek Piety (Oxford 1948) 84-91.

45. E. Coche de la Ferté, La Sculpture grecque et romaine au Musée du Louvre (Paris 1947) 23, 26-27, 439; BrBr 297; H. Bulle, Der Schöne Mensch im Altertum (Leipzig 1912) 343-44, Fig. 86, Pl. 159; A.

Byvanck, "La Chronologie de Praxitèle," Mnemosyne 4 (1951) 204-15,

reported in FA 6 (1951) 108, no. 1400; J. Charbonneaux op. cit.

(supra, n. 23) 10; Encyclopédie photographique de l'art II (ed.

TEL, Paris 1938) 186; A Furtwängler, Masterpieces of Greek Sculpture

(London 1895) 318-20, Fig. 136; G. Lippold, Griechische Plastik

("Handbuch der Archaeolcgie" V, 3, I, ed. W. Otto and R. Herbig,

Munich 1950) 237, Pl. 83, 2; A. Mahler, "Une replique de l'Aphrodite

d'Arles au Musée du Louvre," RA 40, 1 (1902) 301-03, Pl. 12; E.

Michon, "La Vénus d'Arles et sa restauration par Girardon," MonPiot

21 (1913) 13-45, Figs. 1-4; G. Rizzo, Prassitele (Milan and Rome

1932) 24. Other replicas: BrBr 300A; NSc (1925) 162, Pl. 7.

46. O. Broneer, "The Armed Aphrodite on Acrocorinth and the Aphrodite

of Capua," University of California Publications in Classical

Archaeology I, 1 (Berkeley 1930) 65-84, and idem, "Investigations

at Corinth, 1946-47," Hesperia 16 (1947) 233-47, Pl. 64, 28; BrBr

297; J. Charbonneaux op. cit. 9, Fig. 3; A. Furtwängler op. cit.

385-94, Figs. 170-71; G. Lippold op. cit. 284, Pls. 101, 13, and

136, 24; Pausanias (2, 2, 5).

47. L. Alscher, Griechische Plastik III: Nachklassik und Vorhellenismus

(Berlin 1956) 188; M. Bieber, Sculpture of the Hellenistic Age (New

York 1955) 15, 18-20, Figs. 24-27; C. Blinkenberg, Knidia (Copen-

hagen 1933) 231-41, Figs. 53-54, and 201-04, Pl. 4; BrBr 161, 371;

H. Bulle op. cit. 333-7, Pl. 155; L. Caskey op. cit. (supra, n. 25)

68-77, nos. 28, 29; J. Chittenden and C. Seltman, Greek Art, a

Commemorative Catalogue of an Exhibition held in 1946 at the Royal

Academy, Burlington House, London (London 1947) 152, Pls. 4 -41,
(a fine marble copy, c. 150 B.C., Coll. Duke of Bedford); J. Charbonneaux, "L'Aphrodite de Cnide de la collection Kaufmann," Revue
des Arts 1 (1951) 174-76, Figs. 1-4; K. Clark op. cit. (supra, n.
5) 81-87, 383, Figs. 64-65; EA 1633-34, 3068-69, 3782-83, 3784-85,
4938; G. Kaschnitz-Weinberg, Sculture del Magazzino del Museo
Vaticano ("Monumenti Vaticani di archeologia e d'arte" IV, Città
del Vaticano 1936-37) nos. 256-57, Pls. 46-53; C. Kennedy, "Light
and Shade in the Study of Greek Sculpture," (unpublished Ph.D.
dissertation, Dept. of Fine Arts, Harvard University) 9-10; G.
Lippold op. cit. 239, Pl. 83, 3; G. Richter, Handbook (New York
1953) 110, Pl. 88, b, and idem, Sculpture and Sculptors of the
Greeks (rev. ed. New Haven 1950) 260-62, Figs. 668-72 and p. 59;
G. Rizzo op. cit. 48-62, Pls. 82, 86.

48. A. Walters, British Museum: Catalogue of Bronzes in the Department
of Greek and Roman Antiquities (London 1899) 1084, and idem,
British Museum: Select Bronzes, Greek, Roman, and Etruscan, in the
Departments of Antiquities (London 1915) Pl. 45, and idem, British
Museum: Marbles and Bronzes (3d. ed. London 1928) Pl. 48; "A
Statuette of Aphrodite," Bulletin of Rhode Island School of Design
14 (1926) 38-40; G. Richter, "Two Bronze Statuettes," AJA 37 (1933)
48-51, Fig. 1, Pls. 7-8.

49. Necklace -- Pliny (N.H. 34.70); M. Bieber, Antike Skulpturen und
Bronzen in Cassel (Marburg 1915) 149, Pl. 41, and idem, "Die Söhne
des Praxiteles," JdI 38-39 (1923-24) 242-75, Pls. 6-7, and idem,

_Sculpture of the Hellenistic Age_ (New York 1955) 20-21, Fig. 36; W. Klein, "Die Pseliumene des Praxiteles," _JdI_ 9 (1894) 248-50, Pl. 9, and _idem_, _Praxiteles_ (Leipzig 1898) 286-87, and _idem_, _Praxitelische Studien_ (Leipzig 1399) 60-61; F. Poulsen, "Sur la Pseliuméné de Praxiteles," _RA_ 9 (1907) 69-74. Sword -- W. Amelung, _Führer durch die Antiken in Florenz_ (Munich 1897) 52, 75; R. Lullies, _Die kauernde Aphrodite_ (Munich-Pasing 1954) 74-75, Fig. 46.

50. C. Alexander, "A Statue of Aphrodite," _BMMA_ 11 (1953) 241-51 and cover illustration; W. Amelung _op. cit._ 46, 67; M. Bieber, _Sculpture of the Hellenistic Age_ (New York 1955) 20, Figs. 30-31; _BrBr_ 374; H. Bulle _op. cit._ 338-39. Pl. 156; J. Charbonneaux, "La Vénus de Milo et Mithridate le Grand,' _Revue des Arts_ 1 (1951) 10; G. Chase, _Greek and Roman Sculpture in American Collections_ (Cambridge [Mass.] 1924) 140, Fig. 166; K. Clark _op. cit._ 86-87, 383-84, Fig. 67; B. Felletti-Maj. "L'Afrodite pudica, saggio d'arte ellenistica," _ArchCl_ 3 (1951) 41-48, 61-62; A. Furtwängler _op. cit._ 345; F. Johnson, _Lysippos_ (Durham, N.C. 1927) 55, Pls. 9, 36; A. Lawrence _op. cit._ (_supra_, n. 39) 17; G. Lippold _op. cit._ 312; A. Mahler, "Une Hypothèse sur l'Aphrodite de Medicis," _RA_ 41, 1 (1903) 33-38.

51. R. Lullies _op. cit._ 30-62, Fig. 1, p. 38; G. Lippold _op. cit._ 319, Pl. 112, 1.

52. O. Benndorf, "Bemerkungen zur griechischen Kunstgeschichte III: Anadyomene des Apelles," _AM_ 1 (1876) 50-66; O. Brendel, "Weiblicher Torso in Oslo," _Die Antike_ 6 (1930) 41-64, Figs. 1-14, Pls. 7-10; _EA_ 3791; G. Richter, _Catalogue of Greek Sculptures in the Metropolitan Museum of Art_, New York (Cambridge [Mass.] 1954) 85, 152-55;

A. Rumpf, Malerei und Zeichnung ("Handbuch der Archaeologie" VI,
4, 1, Munich 1953) 147, and idem, "Anadyomene," JdI 65-66 (1950-51)
166-74, Figs. 1-2.

53. W. Amelung, Die Sculpturen des Vaticanischen Museums (2 vols.
Berlin 1908) II, 696-98, Gabinetto delle Maschere 433, Pl. 75.

54. R. Carpenter, ArtB 39 (1957) 71; supra, n. 23.

55. R. Lullies and M. Hirmer op. cit. (supra, n. 29) 24-25, Pls. 230-33.

56. H. Winnefeld, Die Friese des grossen Altars ("Altertümer von Pergamon" III, 2, Berlin 1910), Pl. 14.

57. H. Bulle op. cit. (supra, n. 45) 340-42, Fig. 85, Pl. 158; B.
Felletti-Maj. op. cit. (supra, n. 50) 48-54, 62-65; H. Jones, ed.,
Catalogue of the Ancient Sculptures Preserved in the Municipal
Collections of Rome: The Sculpture of the Museo Capitolino (Oxford
1912) Gabinetto della Venere 1, 182-84, Pl. 45.

58. M. Bieber, Sculpture of the Hellenistic Age (New York 1955) 157;
F. Winter, Die Skulpturen ("Altertümer von Pergamon" VII, Berlin
1908) 13-25, no. 22, Pls. 2-4.

59. H. Bulle op. cit. 339-40, Fig. 84, Pl. 157; A. Giuliano op. cit.
(supra, n. 37) 210-44, Pls. 100-101; P. Lévêque, "Notes de sculpture rhodienne (II)," BCH 74 (1950) 62-69, Figs. 2-4, Pl. 13;
J. Marcadé, "Les Trouvailles de la maison dite de l'Hermès à Délos,"
BCH 77 (1953) 563-65, A5631, Fig. 53; H. Michon, "Nouvelles
statuettes provenant d'Égypte," MonPiot 21 (1913) 163-72, Pl. 7;
A. de Vita, "L'Afrodite pudica da Punta delle Sabbie," ArchCl 7
(1955) 9-23, Pls. 5-11.

60. M. Bulard loc. cit. (supra, n. 23), G. Lippold op. cit. (supra, n. 45) 369, Pl. 135, 3.

61. J. Charbonneaux, Revue des Arts 1 (1951) 8-16, Figs. 1, 4, 7-9; K. Clark op. cit. (supra, n. 5) 88-89, 384, Fig. 68; A. Furtwängler op. cit. (supra, n. 45) 367-87, Figs. 158-68; Ency. Phot. de l'art III (Paris 1938) 200-203.

62. S. Aurigemma op. cit. (supra, n. 18) 38, no. 72115, Pl. 39; K. Clark op. cit. 90-93, Fig. 70, cf. Figs. 71-73 of the Three Graces; G. Gullini op. cit. (supra, n. 23) 67-70.

NOTES TO CHAPTER II

1.  J. Bernoulli, Aphrodite (Leipzig 1873) 313-26; W. Klein, Praxiteles
    (Leipzig 1898) 270-72; R. Lullies, Die kauernde Aphrodite (Munich-
    Pasing 1954) 7.  The study presented here was made before the publi-
    cation of the last mentioned book, but it is included here, in
    shortened form, by virtue of its relevance to the remainder of the
    thesis.

2.  R. Paribeni in NSc (1922) 246; G. Battaglia, "L'Afrodite di Doidal-
    sas," BdA 10, 2 (1930-31) 406-16, Figs. 1-7, Pls. 13-14; S. Auri-
    gemma, The Baths of Diocletian and Museo Nazionale Romano (Rome
    1947) 39, no. 108597, Pl. 38b; idem, Le Terme di Diocleziano e il
    Museo Nazionale Romano (Rome 1950) 83, Pl. 38b, Ht. 1.06m.  On the
    continuing importance of the finds at Tivoli, see: A. Van Buren,
    "Recent Finds at Hadrian's Tiburtine Villa," AJA 59 (1955) 214-17,
    Pls. 62-63.

3.  Inv, nos. 2240 and 2241, respectively; for the former, see Encyclo-
    pédie photographique de l'art III (eds. TEL, Paris 1938) 228-29,
    Ht. of both 0.97m.

4.  O. Brendel in EA 3788-90; F. Poulsen, Catalogue of Ancient Sculpture
    in the Ny Carlsberg Glyptothek (Copenhagen 1951) 60, no. 51, Ht.
    0.20m.; W. Amelung, Die Skulpturen des Vaticanischen Museums (2
    vols., Berlin 1903-08) II, 680-84, Gabinetto delle Maschere 427,
    Pl. 76, Ht. 0.83; BrBr 434.

5. J. Bernoulli op. cit. 313-18; W. Klein loc. cit.; O. Kaschnitz-Weinberg, Sculture del Magazzino del Museo Vaticano (Rome 1937) no. 282, Pl. 68; R. Lullies op. cit. 10-16.

6. Jex-Blake and E. Sellers, eds., The Elder Pliny's Chapters on the History of Art (London 1896) 208, line 4 and notes thereto; T. Reinach, "L'Aphrodite au bain," RA 24 (1926) 84-86.

7. "L'Auteur de la 'Vénus accroupie,'" GBA 17, 1, (1897) 314-22.

8. J. Bernoulli op. cit. 323-25; Jex-Blake and E. Sellers op. cit. 208, 239; T. Reinach, GBA 17, (1897) 314-22; W. Klein op. cit. 270; G. Richter, Catalogue of Greek Sculpture in the Metropolitan Museum of Art (Cambridge [Mass.] 1954) 83.

9. J. Bernoulli op. cit. 317; W. Klein op. cit. 272; M. Bernhart, Aphrodite auf griechischen Münzen (Munich 1936) 48-50, nos. 299a-310, Pl. 8; cf. T. Reinach, RA 24 (1926) 84-86; all the coins but one are also illustrated in W. H. Waddington-C. Babelon-T. Reinach, Recueil général des monnaies grecques d'Asie Mineure, vol. I, fasc. I, Pont et Paphlagonie (Paris 1904) 65, 106, Pl. IX, 23; 161, n. 5, Pl. XXII, 4; 164, no. 25, Pl. XXII, 17; 165, no. 32, Pl. XXII, 24. Ibid. fasc. 3, Nicée et Nicomédie, 473, no. 558, Pl. LXXXII, 17; C. Mionnet, Description des médailles antiques grecques et romaines: Supplement, vol. IV (Paris 1829) 21, no. 111, cites one not included above, from Claudiopolis.

10. (Munich 1923) 47-48, cf. T. Reinach loc. cit.

11. S. Reinach, "Deux nouvelles statues d'Aphrodite," MonPiot 27, 2 (1924) 119-39, Figs. 1-9, Pls. 13-15, and especially n. 1, p. 131.

12. M. Bulard, "Aphrodite, Pan et Eros," BCH 30 (1906) 610-31, Pls. 13-16; Waddington-Babelon-Reinach op. cit. vol. I, fasc. 3, 473, no. 588, Pl. 82, 17, a bronze of Severus Alexander from Nicaea shows, in addition to Aphrodite, two Erotes bearing torches, one of whom also holds a mirror.

13. See the account of the shrine by Pliny (N.H. 36.20), analyzed by C. Blinkenberg, Cnidia (Copenhagen 1933), 201-204.

14. W. Amelung, Führer durch die Antiken in Florenz (Munich 1897) 46-47, 67; cf. C. Alexander, "A Statue of Aphrodite," BMMA 11 (1953) 241-51.

15. R. Horn, "Stehende weibliche Gewandstatuen in der hellenistichen Plastik," RM Ergänzungsheft 2 (1931) 19-20, Pl. VI, Fig. 3.

16. M. Bieber, Sculpture of the Hellenistic Age (New York 1955) 66-67, Figs. 214-229.

17. On the Tyche, infra Ch. IV. 80-81.

18. K. Schefold, Untersuchungen zur Kertscher Vasen ("Archäologische Mitteilungen aus russischen Sammlungen" IV, Berlin 1934) 38, 120, Athens 1472, Pl. 38; cf. idem, Kertscher Vasen: no. 3 of Bilder griechischer Vasen ed. Beazley-Jacobsthal (Berlin 1930) Pls. 15-18; W. Züchner, "Griechische Klappspiegel," JdI Ergänzungsheft 14 (Berlin 1942) 46, KS 59, Berlin 8148, from Athens, Pl. 21.

19. R. Lullies, Die kauernde Aphrodite (Munich-Pasing 1954) 50-53, believes it was probably a cult image.

20. R. Horn op. cit. 56-59; R. Carpenter, "Observations on Familiar Statuary in Rome," MAAR 18 (1941) 70-71, S. Aurigemma, National Museum in Rome 35, no. 50170, Pls. 32-33.

21. A. Maiuri and G. Jacopi, Lo Spedale dei Cavalieri e il Museo
    Archeologico di Rhodi (Rhodes 1932) 41, Pl. II; idem, ClRhod
    vol. I, (1928) 22-23, Figs. 5-6.

22. Königliche Museen zu Berlin   Beschreibung der antiken Skulpturen
    (Berlin 1891) 15, no. 23; J. Charbonneaux, "La Vénus de Milo et
    Mithridate le Grand," Revue des Arts 1 (1951) 8-16, Figs. 1-14.

23. L. Caskey, Museum of Fine Arts, Boston:  Catalogue of Greek and
    Roman Sculpture (Cambridge [Mass.] Boston 1925) 71-77, no. 29;
    G. Chase, Greek and Roman Antiquities:  A Guide to the Classical
    Collection (Museum of Fine Arts, Boston 1950) 109-10, Fig. 133;
    A. Lawrence, "Greek Sculpture in Ptolemaic Egypt," JEA 11 (1925)
    179-90, Pls. 18-21.

24. A. Adriani, "L'Afrodite al bagno di Rodi e l'Afrodite di Doedalsas,"
    ASAE 44 (1944) 37-70, Pls. 2-11, Fig. 8; I. Noshy, The Arts in
    Ptolemaic Egypt (London 1937) 96 and n. 2; cf. marble head of the
    crouching Aphrodite type Ht. 0.8 m., reportedly from Alexandria, in
    Report of the Department of Antiquities, Cyprus, 1935 (Nicosia
    1936) 30, Pl. 11, 2; cf. G. Elderkin, "Aphrodite and Artemis as
    Dolls," Art in America 33 (1945) 128-33.

25. L. Caskey op. cit. 68-71, no. 28, and 118-20, no. 56. G. Chase
    op. cit. 94-95, Fig. 108, and 110-11, Fig. 135.

26. Supra, p. 38.

27. A. Levi, Sculture nel Palazzo Ducale di Mantova (Rome 1931) 41,
    no. 64, Pls. 44-45; W. Amelung, Führer durch die Antiken in Florenz
    (Munich 1897) 47-49, no. 68; BrBr., 425; A. Lawrence, Later Greek

Sculpture (New York 1927) 18, Pl. 30, a; M. Bieber, Sculpture of the Hellenistic Age (New York 1955) 110-11, Figs. 438-45. In a long, involved, subjective argument, R. Lullies op. cit. (supra n. 19) 45-48 attempts to insert the Marsyas group into the middle of the second century B.C. It is not convincing.

28. M. Bieber op. cit. 66-67, Figs. 214-229.

NOTES TO CHAPTER III

1. O. Benndorf, "Bemerkungen zur griechischen Kunstgeschichte III:
   Anadyomene des Apelles,"AM I(1876) 50-66; A. Furtwängler, "Aphro-
   dite Diadoumene und Anadyomene," (Helbings) Monatsberichte über
   Kunstwissenschaft und Kunsthandel 1 (1900-01) 177-81, Figs. 1-3,
   Pls. 1-4; G. Perrot, "Une Statuette de la Cyrenaique et l'Aphrodite
   Anadyomène d'Apelle," MonPiot 13 (1906) 117-35, Pl. 10; J. de Mot,
   "La Vénus de Courtrai," MonPiot 21 (1913) 145-62, Pls. 15-16; O.
   Brendel in EA 3791 and "Weiblicher Torso in Oslo," Die Antike 6
   (1930) 41-64, Figs. 1-14, Pls. 7-10; H. Riemann, Kerameikos,
   Ergebnisse der Ausgrabungen 2: Die Skulpturen vom 5. Jahrhundert
   bis in römische Zeit (Berlin 1940) 115-19, no. 170, nude Anadyomene,
   list of 65 examples, no. 172, half-draped type, 48 examples; G.
   Gullini, "Su alcune sculture del tardo Ellenismo," Arti Figurative:
   Rivista d'arte antica e moderna 3 (1947) 61-72, Pls. 32-33; A.
   Rumpf, Malerei und Zeichnung ("Handbuch der Archäologie" V, 4, 1
   Munich 1953) 147 and n. 5; R. Lullies, Die kauernde Aphrodite
   (Munich-Pasing 1954) 76-81, Figs. 48-49; M. Bieber, Sculpture of
   the Hellenistic Age (New York 1955) 98, Figs. 390, 396-97.

2. Jex Blake and E. Sellers, The Elder Pliny's Chapters on the History
   of Art (London 1896) 126-29.

3. R. Lullies loc. cit.

4.  W. Amelung, <u>Die Skulpturen des Vaticanischen Museums</u> (2 vols.
    Berlin 1903-08) II, 696-98, no. 433, Pl. 75; H. Riemann <u>loc</u>. <u>cit</u>.
    On the shape of the navel as characteristic of Hellenistic anatomi-
    cal construction, see B. Felletti-Maj, "Afrodite pudica, saggio
    d'arte ellenistica," <u>ArchCl</u> 1 (1951) 33-65, Pls. 11-13. For
    another example of a navel of inverted triangular shape, deeply
    cut, see A. Furtwängler, <u>Collection Somzée</u> (Munich 1897) 26-27, no.
    35, Pl. 19, v.s. the early third century B.C. deep oval navel of a
    half-draped marble figure from Cos, now in Istanbul, illustrated in
    M. Bieber <u>op</u>. <u>cit</u>. 20; Fig. 32; O. Richter, <u>Catalogue of Greek</u>
    <u>Sculptures in the Metropolitan Museum of Art</u> (Cambridge [Mass.]
    1954) 85, no. 152, here Pl. XLI.

5.  S. Aurigemma, <u>The Baths of Diocletian and Museo Nazionale Romano</u>
    (Rome 1947) 35, no. 50170, Pls. 32-33; M. Bieber <u>op</u>. <u>cit</u>. 40,
    Figs. 97-100.

6.  S. Aurigemma <u>op</u>. <u>cit</u>. 39, no. 108597, Pl. 38; R. Lullies <u>op</u>. <u>cit</u>.
    26, 30-53, Fig. 1.

7.  M. Bieber <u>op</u>. <u>cit</u>. 147-50, emphasizes the priority of sculpture,
    but is not entirely persuasive. A growing body of evidence indi-
    cates many of the Aphrodite motifs were anticipated in vase paint-
    ings of the fourth century B.C., though it is not certain that the
    goddess was depicted. Cnidia - N. Himmelman-Wildschütz, "Zur
    Knidischen Aphrodite I," <u>Marburger Winckelmann-Programm</u> (1957) 11-
    16, Figs. 1-6; <u>Anadyomene</u> - G. Libertine, <u>Il Museo Biscari</u> (Milan
    and Rome 1930) 183-84, no. 768, Pl. 90; Crouching - K. Schefold,

Untersuchungen zu den Kertscher Vasen ("Archäologische Mitteilungen
aus russischen Sammlungen" IV, Berlin 1934) 38, no. 120, Pl. 38.  In
monumental sculpture, the semi-nudity of the half-draped Aphrodite
anadyomene finds ample precedent in the Venus of Arles in the
Louvre, here Pl. I.

8.  H. Walters, British Museum:  Select Bronzes (London 1915) Pl. 45;
    G. Richter, "Two Bronze Statuettes," AJA 37 (1933) 48-51, Fig. 1,
    Pls. 7-8.

9.  BrBr 283; M. Bieber op. cit. 39-40, Fig. 93.

10.  M. Bieber op. cit. 98, Fig. 390, 144, Fig. 610.

11.  Nude anadyomene in Egypt; C. Edgar, Catalogue général des anti-
     quités égyptiennes du Musée du Cairo IV:  Greek Sculpture (Cairo
     1903) 11-12, no. 27454, Pl. 6, here Pl. XXII, cf. nos. 27460, 9305;
     C. Watzinger, Expedition Ernst von Sieglin:  Ausgrabungen in
     Alexandria 1 B (E. Sieglin ed. Leipzig 1927) 71-77, Figs. 25, 27-28;
     on the Dresden example, see A. Greifenhagen, Anz (1933) 428, and
     F. Poulsen, From the Collections of the Ny Carlsberg Glyptothek 2
     (1938) 34; examples no later than c 200 B.C., see A. Ippel, Der
     bronzefund von Galjub:  Modelle eines hellenistischen Goldschmieds
     ("Polizaeusmuseum, Hildesheim, Wissenschaftliche Veröffentlichung
     II," Berlin 1922) 28-29, nos. 7, 8, Pl. 3.  Half-draped examples:
     O. Brendel in EA 3791; Encyclopédie photographique de l'art III
     (Paris 1938) 230A, and E. Michon, "Nouvelles statuettes d'Aphro-
     dite provenant de l'Égypte," MonPiot 21 (1913) 163-72, Pl. 16, here
     Pl. 48; C. Watzinger op. cit. 87-92, no. 72, Fig. 26.  In terra-

cotta, S. de Ricci, "Terres--Cuites greco-egyptiennes," RA 20

(1924) 127-31, Fig. 8. Cf. Isis, A. de Ridder, Les bronzes

antiques du Louvre (2 vols. Paris 1913-15) I, no. 793, Pl. 54, cf.

nos. 789, 790.

12. D. Thompson, "A Portrait of Arsinoë Philadelphos," AJA 59 (1955)

199-206, Pls. 54-55, and 202, note 40; G. Macurdy, Hellenistic

Queens (Baltimore, 1932) 111-30, Figs. 5a, b; cf. H. Jeanmaire, "La

politique religieuse d'Antoine et de Cléopatra," RA 19 (1924) 241-

61, esp. 248-50.

13. A. Levi, Sculture nel Palazzo Ducale di Mantova (Rome 1931) 41,

no. 64, Pls. 44-45.

14. M. Bieber op. cit. 92, 97-98, Figs. 350-53; G. Lippold, Die

griechische Plastik ("Handbuch der Archäologie" V, 3, 1, Munich

1950) 345; OCD, s.v. "Isis," EA 57. Cf. Aphrodite with crown of

Isis, S. Reinach, Répertoire de la sculpture grecque et romaine

(6 vols. Paris 1906-30) II, 362, III, 804, 1. For use of Isis

costume on grave reliefs of the Roman period, see A. Conze, Die

Attischen Grabreliefs (4 vols. Berlin 1893-1922) IV, 54, no. 1954,

Pl. 420; on a terra-cotta of Eros and Psyche, see G. Kleiner,

"Tanagrafiguren," JdI Ergänzungsheft 15 (1942) 248; on a replica of

Eros and Psyche from Memphis, see S. de Ricci, "Groupe en marbre de

la collection Dattari," RA 10 (1907) 103-07. On its widespread use

on late Hellenistic figures, see L. Laurenzi, "Rilievi e statue

d'arte rodia," RM 54 (1939) 42-65, Figs. 1-6, Pls. 11-16, esp. pp.

45-50, Figs. 3-6; cf. Sicilian terra cotta anadyomene as example of spread of the type, NSc (1913) 440; on use of knot on bronze of first century B.C., see W. Lamb, Greek and Roman Bronzes (London 1929) 224-25, Pl. 89a.

15.  N. de G. Davies, The Tomb of Two Sculptors at Thebes (A. Lythgoe ed., "Publications of the Metropolitan Museum of Art Egyptian Expedition, Robb de Peyster Tytus Memorial Series IV," New York 1925) 37-38, 44-46, Pls. 19-21; N. M. Davis and A. H. Gardiner, Ancient Egyptian Painting (2 vols. Chicago 1936) II, Pl. 103; cf. Aphrodite anadyomene invoked as Hathor, E. Drioton, ASAE 45 (1947) 53-98.

16.  R. Horn, "Stehende weibliche Gewandstatuen in der hellenistischen Plastik," RM Ergänzungsheft 2 (1931) 38-39, Pls. 17, 18.

17.  M. Bieber op. cit. 93, Figs. 345, 357-59, respectively; G. Macurdy op. cit., Fig. 6.

18.  O. Brendel in EA 3791.

19.  A. Furtwängler op. cit. (supra, note 1) 180-81, Pl. 3; cf. NSc (1899) 207-08, Fig. 2, nude anadyomene, African marble, navel an inverted triangle, found east of the Basilica in Pompeii.

20.  R. Lullies op. cit. (supra, note 1) 76-81, Figs. 48-49.

21.  S. Aurigemma op. cit. (supra, note 5) 38, no. 72115, Pl. 39; G. Gullini op. cit. (supra, note 1) 67-70.

22.  B. Felletti-Maj op. cit. (supra, note 4) 48-54, 62-65; M. Bulard, "Aphrodite, Pan et Eros: Groupe en marbre," BCH 30 (1906) 610-31, Pls. 13-16, and M. Bieber op. cit. 147-48, Figs. 629-30; G. Pesce, L'Afrodite da Sinvessa (Rome 1939) and National Museum of Naples:

The Archaeological Collections (2d. ed. Naples n.d.) 17, Fig. 43.

23. J. de Mot op. cit. (supra, note 1) 147, Fig. 2; Les antiquités
égyptiennes, grecques, etrusques, romaines et gallo-romaines du
Musée de Mariemont (Brussels 1952) 88, no. G59, Pl. 32; R. Lullies
loc. cit. (supra, note 1).

24. O. Brendel, "Weiblicher Torso in Oslo," Die Antike 6 (1930) 52,
Figs. 5-6; G. Perrot op. cit. (supra, note 1) 117-35, Pl. 10;
H. Riemann op. cit. (supra, note 1) 117-19, listed ffg. no. 172,
no. 39, as half-draped type; now in coll. Mr. and Mrs. Beaumont W.
Wright.

25. J. de Mot op. cit. 145-62, Pls. 14-15; G. Gullini op. cit. 64;
J. Sieveking, Bronzen, Terrakotten, Vasen der Sammlung Loeb (Munich
1930) 16-17, Pl. 14; Walters Art Gallery 48, 1940, unpublished,
according to Dr. D. K. Hill; C. Edgar, Catalogue général des
antiquités égyptiennes du Musée du Cairo VI:  Greek Moulds  (Cairo
1903) 2-3, no. 32004, Pl. 24, reproduced here as Pl. XLVII.

26. Supra, Chapter I, pp. 22-24.

27. B. Felletti-Maj loc. cit.

28. L. Curtius, "Die Aphrodite von Kyrene," Die Antike 1 (1925) 56-60,
Pls. 1-4.

29. A. Furtwängler, La Collection Sabouroff (1883-87) Pl. 37; E. Pfuhl,
"Ikonographische Beiträge zur Stilgeschichte der hellenistischen
Kunst," JdI 45 (1930) 39-40, and note thereto.

30. A. Furtwängler and P. Walters, Beschreibung der Glyptothek zu
München (2d. ed. 1910) 209-16, no. 218; BrBr 4.

31. S. Aurigemma op. cit. (supra, note 5) 39, no. 108597, Pl. 38b;
    F. Poulsen, Catalogue of Ancient Sculpture in the Ny Carlsberg
    Glyptothek (Copenhagen 1951) 60, no. 51; Encyclopédie photographique
    de l'art III (Paris 1938) 228-29.

32. R. Lullies op. cit. (supra, n. 1) 30-39, Fig. 1.

33. R. Carpenter, Review of M. Bieber, Sculpture of the Hellenistic Age
    (New York 1955) in Art3 39 (1957) 71; cf. G. Gullini op. cit.
    (supra, note 21) 67-70

34. M. Bernhart, Aphrodite auf griechischen Münzen (Munich 1936) 33,
    nos. 201, 202, 203, respectively, all illustrated on Pl. 5.

35. OCD, s.v. "Arsinoë II," "Isauria," "Pamphylia," "Ptolemy II,"
    "Ptolemy III," "Phrygia;" D. Thompson op. cit. (supra, note 12)
    199-200; G. Macurdy op. cit (supra, note 12) 111-30, Figs. 5a, b.

36. M. Bernhart op. cit. 44-46, nos. 282, Pl. 8, 283, 284, Pl. 8, 285
    and 275, Pl. 7, 276 and 270, respectively.

37. Ibid., Pruss, no. 283 and the unpublished example in the Newell
    collection of the American Numismatic Society; third century A.D.
    or autonomous, nos. 270, 275, Pl. 7, 276, 282, Pl. 8.

38. Ibid., nos. 287, Pl. 8, 288 and 289, 290, Pl. 8, and 271 and 277,
    Pl. 8, respectively.

39. Ibid., nos. 278, Pl. 8, 281, Pl. 8 and 272, Pl. 7.

40. Ibid., no. 273, Pl. 7; other examples of different types are listed
    on his p. 63 with the archaic, or archaizing, cult image being the
    commonest; see pp. 6-14, nos. 1, 4-10, 18-27, 29-37, 41, 42, Pl. 1,
    44, Pl. 2. Thanks are due Dr Margaret Thompson of the Museum of

the American Numismatic Society for obtaining the illustrations of coins in the Society's collections shown here in Pl. 25.

41. Ibid., 48-50, nos. 299-310, Pl. 8, and supra, Ch. II, n. 9.

42. B. Stark, "Über die unedierten Venusstatuen und das Venusideal seit Praxiteles," Berichte der sächsischen Gesellsch. der Wiss. (1860) 46-97, esp. 77; S. Reinach, "La Vénus d'Alesia," Pro Alesia 1 (1906) 65-71; suggested again by C. Vermeule in his review of R. Lullies, Die kauernde Aphrodite (Munich-Pasing 1954), AJA 60 (1956) 460-63.

1. J. Bernoulli, Aphrodite, ein Baustein für griechische Kunstmythologie (Leipzig 1873) 329–41; A. Furtwängler, La Collection Sabouroff ([n.p.] 1883–87) Pl. 37; E. Pottier and S. Reinach, La necropole de Myrina (2 vols. Paris 1887) I, 285–90, II, 298, Fig. 53, Pl. 55; W. Klein, Praxiteles (Leipzig 1898) 267–70; C. Anti, "Nuove repliche della Venere che si toglie il sandalo," Bollettino del Museo Civico di Padova 20 (1927) 17–38, Figs. 1–6, hereafter "Repliche"; E. Pfuhl, "Ikonographische Beiträge zur Stilgeschichte der hellenistischen Kunst," JdI 45 (1930) 39–40, and n. 1; G. Richter, Metropolitan Museum of Art: Catalogue of Greek Sculptures (Cambridge [Mass.] 1954) 86, no. 156, Pl. 112 d–f; M. Bieber, The Sculpture of the Hellenistic Age (New York 1955) 99 and 144, Figs. 394–95, 606–07.

2. E. Harrison, AJA 61 (1957) 303.

3. C. Anti, "Repliche," 17–21, Figs. 1–3, Ht. 0.193 m.

4. The list is based upon previous ones made by J. Bernoulli op. cit. 330–35 and E. Pottier and S. Reinach op. cit. I, 285–90. Anti's is correlated with illustrations in S. Reinach, Répertoire de la statuaire grecque et romaine (6 vols. Paris 1906–30) I–V, hereafter Répert. stat., but includes a number not illustrated there. For a more recent list see H. Riemann, Kerameikos, Ergebnisse der Ausgrabungen 2: die Skulpturen vom 5. Jahrhundert bis in römische Zeit (Berlin 1940) 113–15.

5. Illustrated in M. Bernhart, <u>Aphrodite auf griechischen Münzen</u> (Munich 1936) 50-51, nos. 311-13, Pl. 8. To Anti's reference for the coin of Aphrodisias in Caria, B. V. Head, <u>BMCC Caria, Cos. Rhodes</u> (London 1897) 31, no. 34, Pl. 5, 14, add J. Friedländer, "Neue Erwerbungen des königlichen Münzkabinets," <u>AZ</u> 26 (1869), Pl. 23, 5, and M. Bernhart 51, no. 313, Pl. 8.

6. Listed in C. Anti, "Postilla alla 'Venere che si toglie il sandalo,'" <u>Bollettino del Museo Civico di Padova</u> 20 (1927) 81-82, nos. 86-89. Continuing his list, add herewith: no. 90, bronze, from Volubilis, now Musée de Volubilis, <u>MonPiot</u> 33 (1933) 111-12, Fig. 5; no. 91, marble from Antioch, now Baltimore Museum of Art, see R. Stillwell, ed. <u>Antioch-on-the-Orontes III: The Excavations, 1937-39</u> (Princeton 1941) 118, no. 266, Pl. 5, Ht. 0.152 m.; no. 92, from Sidon, now private collection, France, reported to have rudder with inscription "the Sidonians," see <u>Guides to the National Museum, Oriental and Classical Antiquity</u> (Copenhagen 1950) 70, 80; no. 93, fragment from Karameikos, marble, see H. Riemann <u>op</u>. <u>cit</u>. 113-14, no. 168, Ht. 0185 m.; no. 94, H. Riemann <u>op</u>. <u>cit</u>. 115, no. 169, Pl. 37, Ht. 0.95 m.; no. 95, in group with Telesphorus, and, originally, Eros, from vicinity of Maidan-Pek, Serbia, bronze, see <u>Les antiquités égyptiennes, grecques, étrusques, romaines et gallo-romaines du Musée de Mariemont</u> (Brussels 1952) 96-97, (G80) 339, Pl. 35, Ht. 0.13 m.

7. C. Anti, "Repliche," 25-26. Their provenience, including probable examples of variant A, was: Western--Italy 5, France 1; Eastern--

Egypt 6, Cyrene 1, Greece 2 (including one from the Aegean), Crete 1, Sidon 1; unknown--4.

8. See one of the copies formerly in the Cook Coll., no. 17 (E. Strong, "The Cook Collection," _JHS_ 28 [1908] 15, Pl. 10), here Pl. XXIV, left, restored as washing her feet with a sponge.

9. C. Anti, "Repliche," 26-29. Western--Italy 8, France 2, Switzerland 1, Algeria 1; Eastern—Egypt 2 (one each, variants B and C), Greece 4, Aegaean 3, coastal Asia Minor 2, Corfu 1, Serbia 1, Syria, Tyre, and Sidon 2, "eastern" 1; unknown--8.

10. Variant D included one Egyptian bronze, whose left arm was extended straight out as far as the elbow and then up, unlike variant C, whose left arm was simply straight; see M. Bieber _op. cit._ (_supra_, note 1) 99, and _Encyclopédie photographique de l'art_ III (Paris 1938) 90-91, Figs, C. D, hereafter _Encyclopédie photographique III_. In variant E, the left arm was pushed against a support. Anti, "Repliche," 29-30, suspected this was an erroneous restoration, see S. Reinach, _Répert. stat._ IV, 214, 8.

11. C. Anti, "Repliche," 34-38.

12. _Ibid._, 34-35; W. Klein _op cit._ (_supra_, note 1) 268; H. Walters, British Museum: _Catalogue of the Bronzes, Greek, Roman and Etruscan, in the Department of Greek and Roman Antiquities_ (London 1899) no. 280, 6-7/8 in., and no. 282, 21-1/2 in., hereafter _Cat. Br._; _idem_, _Select Bronzes, Greek, Roman and Etruscan_ (London 1915) Pls. 25 and 28, hereafter _Sel. Br._

13. H. Walters, _Cat. Br._ no. 282.

14.  C. Anti, "Repliche," 18.

15.  H. Walters, _Cat. Br._ no. 829, Ht. 7-1/2 in., with antique base,
     9-3/4 in.; _idem_. _Sel. Br._ Pl. 43, provenience unknown.

16.  J. De Mot, "L'Aphrodite d'Arenberg," _RA_ 2 (1903) 10-20, Pls. 10-11.
     The supports are generally of two types, either beneath or beside
     the figure.

17.  _Ibid._ 20.

18.  M. Bernhart _loc. cit._ (_supra_, note 5).

19.  A. Furtwängler, _Antike Gemmen_ (2 vols. Leipzig 1900) I, Pl. 43, no.
     42, with rudder, Pl. 44, no. 76, with horn(?).

20.  M. Bieber _op. cit._ 16, Figs. 11-12, and 21, Fig. 39.

21.  R. Lullies and M. Hirmer, _Greek Sculpture_ (New York 1957) 63-64,
     Pl. 189.

22.  F. Johnson, _Lysippos_ (Durham, N.C. 1927) 170-77, Pls. 30-31;
     M. Bieber _op. cit._ 34.

23.  Pliny, _N.H._ 34-65; F. Johnson _op. cit._ 81-91, Pls. 12-13; M. Bieber
     _op. cit._ 31-32, Figs. 74-75; the only copy is in the Vatican, see
     W. Amelung and G. Lippold, _Die Sculpturen des Vaticanischen Museums_
     (3 vols. Berlin 1903-56) III, pt. 1, 86-89, Braccio Nuovo no. 67,
     Pl. II.

24.  W. Amelung and G. Lippold _ibid._, vol. of text III, pt. 2, 314-16,
     vol. of Pls. III, pt. 2, Gall. dei Candelabri Pl. 143; M. Bieber
     _op. cit._ 40, Fig. 102; G. Richter, _Metropolitan Museum of Art:_
     _Greek, Etruscan, and Roman Bronzes_ (New York 1915) 130-31, no. 259.

25. R. Lullies, Die kauernde Aphrodite (Munich-Pasing 1954) 28-29;
    M. Bieber op. cit. 82-83.

26. H. Bulle, Der schöne Mensch im Altertum (2 vols. Munich and Leipzig
    1912) I, 340 and Fig. 84, II, Pl. 157.

27. As shown in M. Bieber op. cit. 73-74, and D. Thompson, "A Bronze
    Dancer from Alexandria,' AJA 54 (1950) 375.

28. Encyclopédie photographique III 234-35, A. B; M. Bieber op. cit.
    81-82, Fig. 285 (example in Museo Capitolino), omitted from her
    list is a marble replica in the Musée d'Art et d'Histoire, Geneva,
    illustrated in W. Deonna, Choix de monuments de l'art antique
    (Geneva 1923) no. 17.8944.

29. E. Pfuhl op. cit. (supra, note 1) 39-40, and n. 1.

30. J. De Mot op. cit. (supra, note 16) 10-20, Pls. 10-11.

31. M. Bieber op. cit. (supra, note 1) 99.

32. Supra, note 10.

33. Supra, note 7.

34. C. Edgar, Catalogue général des antiquités égyptiennes du Musée du
    Caire IV: Greek Sculpture (Cairo 1903) vii, 12, no. 27456, Pl. 6.

35. D. Thompson op. cit. (supra, note 27) 371-85, Figs. 1-3, 11, 14;
    D. von Bothmer, Greek, Etruscan, Roman Antiquities, An Exhibition
    from the Collection of Walter Cummings Baker, Esq. (New York 1950)
    9, no. 46; Ancient Art in American Private Collections:  a Loan
    Exhibition at the Fogg Art Museum of Harvard University (Cambridge
    1954) 32, no. 221, Pl. 67.

36. C. Edgar op. cit. 12, no. 27457, Pl. 6.

37. G. Richter, Greek Br. 74-77, no. 121.

38. Cf. a figure of Hypnos(?), see D. von Bothmer op. cit. 9, no. 45, and Ancient Art in Amer. Priv. Colls. (1954) 32, no. 222, Pl. 68.

39. Encyclopédie photographique III, 230-31, B, C; M. Bieber op. cit. 112, Fig. 623 (Louvre) and Fig. 625 (Mus. Naz. Rome). It is not without significance that the Hermaphrodite's coiffure has the same "S" curved forelock discussed here. On transparent drapery, D. Thompson loc. cit. (supra, note 35) has shown that this style commences prior to the middle of the third century B.C., while still agreeing on its greater prevalence in the second.

40. Königliche Museen zu Berlin: Beschreibung der antiken Skulpturen (Berlin 1891) 15, no. 23; A. Furtwängler, Sabouroff, Pl. 37, Parian marble, from Aegion, Ht. 0.64 m.

41. Cf. the Bartlett head coiffure, L. Caskey, Museum of Fine Arts, Boston: Catalogue of Greek and Roman Sculpture (Cambridge [Mass.] 1925) 68-71, no. 28.

42. E. Pfuhl op. cit. (supra, note 1) 39-40, n. 1; OCD, s.v. "Priapus."

43. E. Strong op. cit. (supra, note 8) 15, no. 17, Pl. 10, Ht. 0.35 m., including pedestal; head and torso only are antique.

44. L. Caskey op. cit. 71-77, no. 29.

45. G. Jacobi, Lo spedale dei cavalieri e il Museo Archeologico di Rhodi (Rome 1932) 41, Pl. 2.

46. B. Head op. cit. (supra, note 5) 31, no. 34, Pl. 5, 11, and 14, Pl. 7, 3. The coins illustrated here are in the collection of the American Numismatic Society. I am indebted to Dr. Margaret Thompson, Curator of Greek Coins, for the photographs.

47. M. Bernhart op. cit (supra, note 5) 50-51, no. 311, Pl. 8, Commodus, and 312, Pl. 8, Gordian III, and 313, Pl. 8, autonomous issue of Aphrodisias.

48. No. 97.357, Ht. 0.374 π.; F. Winter, Typen der figürlichen Terrakotten (vol. III, pt. 2 of "Die antiken Terrakotten," Berlin 1903) 206, 3.

49. Ibid., 205, 7, and 207, 5, from Magna Graecia and Sicily.

50. Ibid., 205, 6, 206, 3, 207, 2, totalling six; E. Pottier and S. Reinach op. cit. (supra, note 1) I, 285-90, II, 298, Fig. 53, Pl. 55.

51. D. Burr, Terra-Cottas from Myrina in the Museum of Fine Arts, Boston (Vienna 1934) 5.

52. G. Kleiner, "Tanagrafiguren," JdI Ergänzungsheft 15 (1942) lists none.

53. Ibid., 218, there dated after 150 B.C.; T. Wiegand, H. Schrader et al., Priene, Ergebnisse der Ausgrabungen und Untersuchungen in den Jahren 1875-1898 (Berlin 1904) 336, Fig. 377, base restored, Ht. 0.32 m.

54. Nat'l. Mus. Athens 4864; F. Winter op. cit. 206, 3; G. Kleiner op. cit. 218, has it precede the Priene piece.

55. F. Winter op. cit. 207, 1; another statuette from Tripoli in Syria, of the "Pselimmene" type, with Eros, is illustrated in BAntFr 8 (1897) Pl. opp. p. 264.

56. C. Edgar, Catalogue général des antiquités égyptiennes du Musée du Caire VI: Greek Moulds (Cairo 1903) 2-3, nos. 32004-09, Pls. 1, 24.

57. E. Pottier and S. Reinach op. cit. I, 269, no. 18, II, Pl. 3.

58. Arndt-Amelung EA 1396.

59. M. Bieber op. cit. (supra, note 1) 111, Fig. 449; A. Furtwängler, "Der Satyr aus Pergamon," Winckelmann's Programm 40 (Berlin 1880) Pl. 1; cf. dancing Silenus related to this satyr, found with an Aphrodite binding her sandal, see L. Chatelain, "L'Éphèbe versant à boire de Volubilis," MonPiot 33 (1933) 107-11, Figs. 1, 2, 5.

60. A. Merlin, "Statuettes de bronzes trouvées en mer près de Mahdia," MonPiot 18 (1910) 15-16, Pl. 5; M. Bieber op. cit. 111-12.

61. G. Richter, Metropolitan Museum of Art: Handbook of the Greek Collection (Cambridge [Mass.] 1953) 125, Pl. 104b; M. Bieber op. cit. 112, Fig. 447.

62. G. Richter, Handbook (1953) 125, Pl. 104c; M. Bieber op. cit. 112, Fig. 448.

63. W. Klein, "Die Aufforderung zum Tanz: eine wiedergewonnene Gruppe des antiken Rokoko," Zeitschrift für bildende Kunst 20 (1908-09) 101-12, Figs. 1-10; M. Bieber op. cit. 139, Figs. 562-67.

64. S. Reinach, "La Vénus d'Alesia," ProAlesia 1 (1906) 70-71; K. Jex-Blake and E. Sellers, The Elder Pliny's Chapters on the History of Art (London 1896) 206-09.

65. L'Auteur de la 'Vénus accroupie,'" GBA 17 (1897) 314-22.

66. G. Lippold, Kopien and Umbildungen griechischer Statuen (Munich 1923) 47-48.

67. S. Reinach loc. cit.

68. K. Stark, "Ueber unedierte Venusstatuen und das Venusideal seit
   Praxiteles," <u>Berichte der Sächsischen Gesellsch. der Wiss.</u> (1860)
   46-97, esp. 77-80.

NOTES TO CHAPTER V

1. A. Lawrence, "Cessavit ars: Turning Points in Hellenistic Sculpture," RA 31-32 (1949) 581-86.

2. Still in use in the 1920's, see G. Chase, Greek and Roman Sculpture
   in American Collections (Cambridge [Mass.] 1924).

3. K. Schefold, Untersuchungen zu den Kertscher Vasen ("Archäologische
   Mitteilungen aus russischen Sammlungen" 4, Berlin
   1934) Pl. 38.

4. G. Libertine, Il Museo Biscari (Milan, Rome 1930) 183-84, Pl. 90,
   no. 768.

5. B. Felletti-Maj, "Afrodite pudica: Saggio d'arte ellenistica,"
   ArchCl 3 (1951) 33-65, Pls. 11-13; H. Stuart Jones, A Catalogue of
   the Ancient Sculptures Preserved in the Municipal Collections of
   Rome: The Sculptures of the Museo Capitolino, (Oxford 1912)
   Gabinette della Venere, 1, 182-84, Pl. 45; W. Amelung, Führer durch
   die antiken in Florenz (Munich 1897) 46, no. 67.

6. Encyclopédie photographique de l'art III (Paris 1938) 226-27.

7. D. Thompson, "A Bronze Dancer from Alexandria," AJA 54 (1950)
   371-385, Figs. 1-17, esp, 380 and notes thereto, Figs. 11, 13; M.
   Bieber, Sculpture of the Hellenistic Age (New York 1955) 132-33,
   Figs. 522-23, 525; Encyclopedie photographique III, 2490, 252A.

8. G. Krahmer, "Die einansichtige Gruppe und die späthellenistische Kunst," GöttNachr (1927) 5?-91; G. Marconi, "Gruppe erotici del ellenismo nei musei di Roma," BullComm 31 (1923) 225-98, Figs. 1-8, Pls. 1-2; A. Schober, "Eine neue Satyrgruppe," RM 52 (1937) 83-93, Fig. 1, Pls. 23-26.

9. M. Bieber op. cit. 113-18, Figs. 458-70.

10. M. Bieber op. cit. 120-21, Figs. 477-78.

11. K. Clark, The Nude, a Study in Ideal Form (New York 1956) 84-86, Fig. 66.

12. R. Carpenter, "Observations on Familiar Statuary in Rome," MAAR 18 (1941) 73-81.

13. B. Felletti-Maj op. cit. (supra, n. 5) 49-53.

14. G. Richter, Metropolitan Museum of Art: Handbook of the Greek Collection (Cambridge [Mass.] 1953) 110, Pl. 88a.

15. W. Amelung loc. cit. (supra, n. 5).

16. W. Amelung, Die Skulpturen des Vaticanischen Museums (2 vols. Berlin 1908) II, 696-98, Gabinetto delle Maschere 433, Pl. 75.

17. M. Bulard, "Aphrodite, Pan et Éros: Groupe en marbre," BCH 30 (1906) 610-31, Pls. 13-16; G. Krahmer, "Stilphasen der hellenistischen Plastik," RM 38-39 (1923-24) 183 and n. 5; ibid., GöttNachr (1927) 66, 89; A. Lawrence, Later Greek Sculpture and Its Influence on East and West (London 1927) 38-39, Pl. 63.

18. E. Pfuhl, "Ikonographische Beiträge zur Stilgeschichte der hellenistischen Kunst," JdI 45 (1930) 39-40 and note thereto.

19. C. Blinkenberg, Knidia (Copenhagen 1933) 82-83; Encyclopédie photographique III, 226-27.

20. Königliche Museen zu Berlin: Beschreibung der antiken Skulpturen (Berlin 1891) 15, no. 23.

21. H. Winnefeld, Die Friese des grossen Altars ("Altertümer von Pergamon" III, 2, Berlin 1910) Pl. 14. The Capitoline type's popularity in Roman times is indicated by her use in portraiture, unseemly as this may appear to modern taste; see, G. Richter, "Who Made the Roman Portrait Statues -- Greeks or Romans?" ProcPhilSoc 95 (1951) 187, Fig. 14.

22. B. Felletti-Maj op. cit. 54-56, 65, Pl. 13, 1.

23. C. Anti, "La Venere 'Maliziosa' di Cirene," Daedalo 6 (1925-26) 683-701, eight illus. in text; B. Felletti-Maj op. cit. 58-61, Pl. 13, 2; G. Richter, Three Critical Periods in Greek Sculpture (Oxford 1951) 47-48, and notes thereto.

24. G. Richter, Handbook 110, Pl. 88b.

25. M. Bieber op. cit. (supra, n. 7) 144, Fig. 608; E. Michon, "Nouvelles statuettes d'Aphrodite provenant de l'Égypte," MonPiot 21 (1913) 163-72, Pl. 17.

26. A. Furtwängler, Masterpieces of Greek Sculpture (London 1895) 318-22, Fig. 137; R. Horn, "Stehende weibliche Gewandstatuen in der hellenistischen Plastik," RM Ergänzungsheft 2 (1931) 54; R. Lullies, Die kauernde Aphrodite (Munich-Pasing 1954) 67; A. Smith, A Catalogue of Sculpture in the Department of Greek and Roman Antiquities of the British Museum (3 vols. London 1892-1904) III, no. 1574.

27. G. Krahmer, RM 38-39 (1923-24) 177; R. Horn op. cit. 49-61, Pls. 18-21.

28. M. Bieber op. cit. 133, Fig. 527; G. Jacobi, "L'Afrodite pudica del Museo archeologico di Rodi," BdA 9 (1929-30) 401-09, Figs. 1-9; idem., ClRhod V, 1 (1931) 5-15, Figs. 1-8, Pl. 1; idem., Lo Spedale dei Cavalieri e il Museo archeologico di Rodi (Rome 1932) 49-50, Pl. 3; P. Lévêque, "Notes de sculpture rhodienne (II)," BCH 74 (1950) 62-69, Figs. 2-4, Pl 13; A. de Vita, "L'Afrodite pudica da Punta delle Sabbie," ArchCl 7 (1955) 9-23, Pls. 5-11. Comparable examples -- L. Laurenzi, "Sculture inedite del Museo di Coo," ASAtene 33-34, N.S. 17-18 (1955-56) 82-83, no. 21, Fig. 21; J. Marcadé, "Les Trouvailles de la maison dite de l'Hermès à Délos," BCH 77 (1953) 563-65, no. A5631, Fig. 53; E. Michon, "Trois Aphrodites ayant appartenu à Joseph Durighello," Syria 6 (1925) 306-09, Pl. 38.

29. Supra, note 20.

30. G. Jacobi, BdA 9 (1929-30) 401-09; P. Lévêque loc. cit.

31. A. de Vita op. cit. 22-23.

32. H. Bulle, Der schöne Mensch im Altertum (2 vols. Munich and Leipzig 1912) 337-40, Fig. 84, Pl. 157; A. Giuliano, "La Afrodite Callipige di Siracusa," ArchCl 5 (1953) 210-14, Pls. 100-103; H. Riemann, Kerameikos: Ergebnisse der Ausgrabungen 2: Die Skulpturen vom 5. Jahrhundert bis in römische Zeit (Berlin 1940) 124; cf. Encyclopédie photographique III, 225.

33. W. Amelung, Vaticanischen Museums II, 712-14, Gabinetto delle Maschere 441, Pl. 75; M. Bieber op. cit. 144, Fig. 610.

34. G. Richter, Catalogue of Greek Sculptures in the Metropolitan Museum of Art (Cambridge [Mass.] 1954) 85, no. 152, Pl. 110.

35. A. Adriani, "L'Afrodite al bagno di Rodi e l'Afrodite di Doedalsas," ASAE 44 (1944) 37-70, Fig. 1, Pls. 2-11; idem. "Contributo allo studio dell' Afrodite di Doedalsas," BSRAA 39 (1951) 144-81; C. Jacobi, Lo Spedale dei Cavalieri e il Museo archeologico di Rodi (Rome 1932) 41, Pl. 2; L. Laurenzi, "La personalità di Doedalsas di Bitinia," ASAtene 24 (1946-48) 167-79; R. Lullies op. cit. (supra, note 26) 83-85; A. Maiuri and C. Jacobi, ClRhod 1 (1927) 22-26, Figs. 5-6. Cf. E. de Miro, "Statuette di Afrodite accoccolata al Museo di Agrigento," ArchCl 8 (1956) 48-52, Pl. 18.

36. L. Caskey, Museum of Fine Arts, Boston: Catalogue of Greek and Roman Sculpture (Cambridge [Mass.] 1925) 71-77, no. 29.

37. G. Gullini, "Su alcune sculture del tardo ellemismo," Arti Figurative 3 (1947) 61-72, Pls. 32-33; J. de Mot, "La Vénus de Courtrai," MonPiot 21 (1913) 145-62, K. Neugebauer, "Die Venus von Grenoble," Pantheon 17 (1936) 50-54, Figs. 1-6; G. Richter, "Two bronze statuettes, AJA 37 (1933) 48-51, Pls. 7-8.

38. M. Bieber op. cit. (supra, note 7) 98, cf. Fig. 390; C. Edgar, Catalogue général des antiquités égyptiennes du Musee du Caire I: Greek Sculpture (Cairo 1903) 11-12, no. 27454, Pl. 6; A. Lawrence, "Greek Sculpture in Ptolemaic Egypt," JEA 11 (1925) 183.

39. G. Dickens, *Hellenistic Sculpture* (Oxford 1920) 33, Fig. 25; A. Greifenhagen *AA* (1933) 428. P. Herrmann, *Verzeichnis der antiken original-Bildwerke* ("Skulpturen-Sammlung," Dresden 1915) 48–49, no. 196; A. Lawrence *op. cit*. 183, Pl. 20; R. Lullies *op. cit*. 67; F. Poulsen, "Gab es eine alexandrinische Kunst?" *From the Collections of the Ny Carlsberg Glyptottek* (Copenhagen 1938) 34; W. Zschietz-schmann, *Die hellenistische und römische Kunst* ("Handbuch der Kunstwissenschaft II," 2, Potsdam 1939) 32, Fig. 20.

40. *Encyclopédie photographique* III, 230A; E. Michon *op. cit*. (*supra*, note 25) 163-72, Pl. 16.

41. C. Edgar, *Catalogue général des antiquités égyptiennes du Musée du Caire VI: Greek Moulds* (Cairo 1903) 2-3, no. 32004, Pl. 24, reproduced here as Pl. XLVII,

42. On the discovery, see C. Perrot, "Une Statuette de la Cyrénaique et l'Aphrodite Anadyomène d'Apelle," *MonPiot* 13 (1906) 117-35, Pl. 10; on the type, perhaps deliberately made with a smooth cut, complete or to be placed on a draped lower portion, see O. Brendel, "Weibli-cher Torso in Oslo," *Die Antike* 6 (1930) 41-64, Figs. 1-14, esp. 5-6, and Pls. 7-10. The present owners are Mr. and Mrs. Beaumont W. Wright.

43. M. Bieber *op. cit*. 98, Figs. 396-97; G. Bagnani, "Hellenistic Sculpture at Cyrene," *JHS* 41 (1921) 232-35; G. Gullini *op. cit*. 67-70; L. Mariani, "L'Afrodite di Cirene," *BdA* 8 (1914) 177-184, two plates in text; cf. figurine with dolphin of the same type, indifferent quality, from Smyrna, L. Caskey *op. cit*. (*supra*, note 36) 173, no. 96.

44. L. Curtius, "Die Aphrodite von Kyrene," Die Antike 1 (1925) 36-60, Figs. 1-18, Pls. 1-4.

45. R. Carpenter, in a review of M. Bieber, Sculpture of the Hellenistic Age (New York 1955), ArtB 39 (1957) 67-73.

46. K. Neugebauer op. cit. (supra, note 37) 50-54, Figs. 1-6.

47. M. Bieber op. cit. (supra, note 7) 148-48, Figs. 629-30; M. Bulard op. cit. (supra, note 17) 610-31, Pls. 13-16; G. Krahmer, RM 38-39 (1923-24) 183; G. Lippold, Kopien und Umbildungen griechischer Statuen (Munich 1923) 33. The back of the Aphrodite of Melos: Encyclopedie photographique III, 201.

48. G. Bagnani loc. cit. (supra, note 43) G. Becatti, "Timarchides e l'Apollo qui tenet Citharam," BullComm 63 (1935-36) 111-31, Figs. 1-9, Pls. 1-2; M. Bieber op. cit. 160, Figs. 678-79; A. Smith op. cit. (supra, note 26) II, 222-25, no. 1380.

49. V. Cianfarani, "Sculture rinvenuti negli scavi di Alba Fucense," BdA 36 (1951) 246-47, Figs. 1-3; F. de Visscher, "Les Fouilles d'Alba Fucens de 1951-1953," AntCl 24 (1955) 100-105, Pls. 39-45. A statue which is similar to the same figure is illustrated in R. Lullies, Die kauernde Aphrodite (Munich-Pasing 1954) Figs. 48-49.

50. G. Richter, Metropolitan Museum of Art: Greek, Etruscan, and Roman Bronzes (New York 1915) 74-77, no. 121; ibid. Handbook 110, Pl. 88b.

51. G. Richter, Catalogue of Greek Sculptures (1954) 83, and supra, Chapter III.

52. G. Pesce, L'Afrodite da Sinvessa (Rome 1939); National Museum of Naples: The Archaeological Collections (2d. ed. Naples n.d.) 17, Fig. 43.

53. For characteristic work of this time from Rhodes, see ClRhod I (1927) 24-25, Figs. 5-6, V, 2 (1932) 30-31, Figs. 19-21, Pls. 3-4 and 143-47, Figs. 34-35, Pl. 15, IX (1938) 50-51, Fig. 31. On the same style at Cos, see L. Laurenzi in ASAtene 33-34, N.S. 17-18 (1955-56) 59-156, esp. 64-65, no. 1, 82-87, nos. 16-31, 121, no. 130, 129-31. For the sfumato style at Alexandria, see A. Adriani in ASAE 44 (1944) 37-70, Fig. 1, Pls. 2-11, and in Arti Figurative 3 (1947) 58. On the development of sfumato, see B. Felletti-Maj op. cit. (supra, note 5) 45, note 4. On its appearance in Sicily, see E. de Miro op. cit. (supra, note 35) 48-52, Pl. 18; cf. A. Giuliano op. cit. (supra, note 32) 210-14, Pls. 100-103.

54. G. Richter, Three Critical Periods in Greek Sculpture (Oxford 1951) 67-70.

55. R. Horn op. cit. (supra, note 26) 76-78; G. Lippold, Griechische Plastik ("Handbuch der Archäologie" V, 3, 1, Munich 1950) 364-74.

56. M. Bieber op. cit. (supra, note 7) 133; G. Chase op. cit. (supra, note 2) 145.

57. M. Bieber op. cit. 133, Figs. 528-29; A. Maiuri in ClRhod V, 2 (1932) 30-31, no. 38, Figs. 19-21, Pls. 3-4, cf. G. Gullini op. cit. (supra, note 37) 64-66, Pl. 33.

58. Cf. the so-called Aphrodite diadoumene: M. Bieber op. cit. 144, Figs. 604-05; H. Bulle op. cit. (supra, note 52) 331, 688, Pl. 153;

A. Furtwängler, "Aphrodite Diadumene und Anadyomene," (Helbings)
Monatsberichte über Kunstwissenschaft und Kunsthandel 1 (1900)
177-81, Figs. 1-3, Pls. 1-4.

59. G. Chase loc. cit. and Fig. 171; Worcester Art Museum Annual 2
(1936-37) 12, Fig. 12.

60. M. Bieber op. cit. 147-48, Figs. 629-30, cf. Fig. 432; M. Bulard
op. cit. (supra, note 17) 610-31, Pls. 13-16; S. Reinach, Musée de
St.-Germain-en-Laye: Bronzes figurés de la Gaule romaine (Paris
n.d.) 61, no. 45; idem, "Aphrodite et Éros: Groupe de Myrina au
Musée d'Athènes," RA 1 (1903) 205-12, Pl. 3; H. Walters, British
Museum: Select Bronzes (London 1915) Pl. 46.

61. M. Bieber op. cit. 159-60, Figs. 673-75; J. Charbonneaux, "La Vénus
de Milo et Mithridate le Grand," Revue des Arts 1 (1951) 8-16,
Figs. 1-14; K. Clark op. cit. (supra, note 11) 88-89, Fig. 68:
Encyclopédie photographique III, 200-203; A. Furtwängler op. cit.
(supra, note 26) 367-401, Figs. 158-76; G. Krahmer, RM 38-39 (1923-
24) 138-41, and 149, n. 1; L. Laurenzi in ClRhod V, 2 (1932) 148-50,
no. 13.621, Fig. 36, and in RivIstArch 8 (1940) 33-36, Figs. 6-8;
A. Lawrence, Later Greek Sculpture (1927) 35-37.

62. T. Homolle, "Statue de Caius Ofellius: sur une oeuvre signée des
artistes Dionysios et Polyclès," BCH 5 (1881) 390-96, Pl. 12; E.
Lapalus, L'Agora des Italiens ("L'Exploration archéologique de
Délos 19: L'École franç. d'Athènes," Paris 1939) 41-60; A. Lawrence
op. cit. 34, Pls. 57, 58a.

63. M. Bieber op. cit. 157-59. Figs. 665-72.

64. O. Broneer, "The Armed Aphrodite on Acrocorinth and the Aphrodite of Capua," University of California Publications in Classical Archaeology 1 (Berkeley 1950) 65-84; BrBr 297; J. Charbonneaux, Revue des Arts 1 (1951) 9, Fig. 3; A. Furtwängler op. cit. 385-94, Figs. 170-71; G. Lippold op. cit. (supra, note 55) 284, Pls. 101, 13 and 136, 24; Pausanias (2.2.5).

65. J. Charbonneaux, Revue des Arts 1 (1951) 11; E. Langlotz, Phidias-probleme (Frankfurt am Main 1947) 83, Pl. 26; C. Picard, Manuel d'archéologie greccue, la sculpture II: Période classique - Ve siècle (one vol. in two pts. Paris 1939) pt. 1, 342-44, Fig. 146; H. Schrader, Pheidias (Frankfurt am Main 1924) 73-74, Fig. 57, 266, Fig. 243.

66. L. Caskey op. cit. (supra, note 36) 68-71, no. 28. Compare illustration on p. 70, right profile, with same view of Melos head, Encyclopédie photographique III, 203.

67. J. Charbonneaux, Revue des Arts 1 (1951) 16.

68. Ibid. 12-16, Figs. 2, 7-14.

1. G. Gullini, "Su alcune sculture del tardo Ellenismo," Arti Figurative 3 (1947) 67-70.

2. L. Laurenzi, "Rilievi e statue d'arte rodia," RM 54 (1939) 42-65,
   Figs. 1-6, Pls. 11-16.

3. C. Fredrich, "Die Aphrodite von Aphrodisias in Karien," AM 22
   (1897) 361-80, Pl. 12; G. Lippold, Die griechische Plastik
   ("Handbuch der Archäologie V, 3, 1, Munich 1950) 377 and n. 4; cf.
   M. Abramic, in "Antike Kopien griechischer Skulpturen in Dalmatien,"
   Festschrift für Rudolf Egger (3 vols. Klagenfurt 1952-54) I, 315-
   18, Fig. 4a, b; and "Die 'asiatische Aphrodite' aus Virunum," ibid.
   III, 135-38; L. Robert and J. Robert, La Carie, histoire et
   géographie historique avec le recueil des inscriptions antiques II:
   Le plateau de Tabai et ses environs (Paris 1954) 25 and n. 1. For
   the image on coins, see M. Bernhart, Aphrodite auf griechischen
   Münzen (Munich 1936) 6-14, nos. 1-44, Pls. 1-2, esp. pp. 7, 10, no.
   21, Pl. 1. The coin illustrated here is in the Museum of the
   American Numismatic Society, New York, and is reproduced through
   the courtesy of Dr. Margaret Thompson, Curator of Greek Coins.

4. G. Bagnani, "Hellenistic Sculpture at Cyrene," JHS 41 (1921) 232-
   46, Figs. 1-5, Pls. 17, 18; G. Becatti, "Le tre grazie," BullComm
   65 (1937) 41-60, Figs. 1-12, Pls. 1-4; M. Bieber, Sculpture of the

Hellenistic Age (New York 1955) 149-50; W. Deonna, "Le groupe des trois graces nues et sa descendance," RA 31 (1930) 274-332, Figs. 1-7.

5. R. Lullies, "Zur drei-Grazien-Gruppe," MdI 1 (1948) 45-52; M. Schmidt, "Über einige Fälle der Übertragung gemalter Figuren in Rundplastik," Festschrift für Paul Arndt (Munich 1925) 103-114.

6. M. Bulard, "Aphrodite, Pan et Éros: Groupe en marbre," BCH 30 (1906) 610-31, Pls. 13-16; cf. H. Beyen, Die pompejanische Wanddekoration vom zweiten bis zum vierten Stil (2 vols. The Hague 1938) I, 288-90, II, Fig. 130, Aphrodite, here clothed and crowned, with Pan and Eros, who are being chastised by the goddess; G. Lippold op. cit. 369, Pl. 135, 3.

7. J. Charbonneaux, "Le geste de la Vénus de Milo," Revue des Arts 6 (1956) 105-06, Figs. 1-4. He rejects the assumption made by L. Laurenzi in RivIstArch 8 (1940) 33ff., according to Charbonneaux, and cites G. Lippold op. cit. 284, who compares the statue of Aphrodite and Eros to the Capua Aphrodite. On the figure suggested, see L. Laurenzi in ClRhod V, 2 (1932) 148-50, no. 13621, Fig. 36, there dated to first century A.D. Cf. female figure, possibly Aphrodite, leaning on herm, of terra-cotta, K. Schefold, "Zwei tarentinische Meisterwerke," MusHelv 8 (1951) 171-76, Figs. 1-4; for another late Hellenistic type with Eros, see NSc (1939) 439-49.

8. M. Bieber op. cit. 166, Figs. 710-11; R. Horn, "Stehende weibliche Gewandstatuen in der hellenistischen Plastik," RM Ergänzungsheft 2 (1931) 89, Pl. 37, 3.

9. A thesis advanced by L. Laurenzi, "Lineamenti d'arte ellenistica," _Arti Figurative_ 1 (1945) 13-28, Pls. 1-9. On the Laocoon, see M. Bieber _op_. _cit_. 134-35, Figs. 530-33, and notes 69-72, her Fig. 530 is the Dresden restoration; for a painting of the subject, see A. Maiuri, _La casa del Menandro e il tesoro di argenteria_ (2 vols. Rome 1933) I, 41, II, Pl. 4; as a replica of a painting, see G. Lippold _op_. _cit_. 384, Pl. 135, 2; on a proposed date of c. 150 B.C., see G. Richter, _Three Critical Periods in Greek Sculpture_ (Oxford 1951) 67-70.

10. W. Amelung, _Führer durch die antiken in Florenz_ (Munich 1897) 46, 67; C. Alexander, "A Statue of Aphrodite," _BMMA_ 11 (1953) 241-51 and cover illustration.

11. M. Bieber, "Die Venus Genetrix des Arkesilaos," _RM_ 48 (1933) 261-76, Figs. 1-4. On the type commonly called the Genetrix, see C. Picard, _Manuel d'archéologie grecque II, la sculpture: Période classique--Ve. siècle_ (1 vol. in 2 pts. Paris 1939) 620-23, Figs. 247-51. A recent study of Venus is reviewed by the same author in _RA_ 48 (1956) 112-14; R. Schilling, _La religion romaine de Vénus depuis les origines jusqu'aux temps d'Auguste_ (Paris 1954) cf. A. Ernout, "Venus, venia, Cupido," _RevPhil_ 30 (1956) 7-27; A. Bartoli, "Il culto della Mater Deum Magna Idaea e di Venere Genetrice sul Palatino," _MemPontAcc_ 6 (1947) 229-39, relates her worship to reverence for Aeneas and the origin of Rome.

12. R. Carpenter in _MAAR_ 18 (1941) 30-35, Pls. 13, 14; J. Charbonneaux, "Torse féminin du type de la Vénus de l'Esquilin' au Musée du

Louvre," _MonPiot_ 39 (1943) 35-48, Fig. 1, Pls. 4-5; H. Jones,

_A Catalogue of the Ancient Sculptures Preserved in the Municipal_

_Collections of Rome: The Sculptures of the Palazzo Conservatori_

(Oxford 1926) 150-53, no. 37, Pl. 54. Its similarity to dolls of

the fifth century B.C. does not outweigh its artificiality as a

later pastiche, see B. Schweitzer, "Eine attische Tonpuppe," _RM_ 44

(1929) 1-25, Figs. 1-3, Pls. 1-5.

13. This thesis runs throughout H. Focillon, _The Life of Forms in Art_,

trans. C. Hogan and G. Kubler (New Haven 1942); it may be con-

trasted with the special study of architectural forms in the seven-

teenth-eighteenth centuries by S. Fiske Kimball, _The Creation of_

_the Rococo_ (Philadelphia 1943).

14. W. Klein, Vom antiken Rokoko (Vienna 1921).

15. A. Furtwängler and P. Wolters, _Beschreibung der Glyptothek zu_

_München_ (2d. ed. Munich 1910) 209-16, no. 218; R. Lullies and M.

Hirmer, Greek Sculpture (New York 1957) 75, Pls. 234-35; G. Richter,

_Metropolitan Museum of Art: Handbook of the Greek Collection_

(Cambridge [Mass.] 1953) 123-24, no. 43.11.4, Pl. 102, for the

life-size figure presumed to be the original, and no. 13.225.2,

Pl. 103b, for a small replica, motive reversed.

16. _Supra_, Chapter IV, 82-87; E. Pfuhl, "Ikonographische Beiträge zur

Stilgeschichte der hellenistischen Kunst," _JdI_ 45 (1930) 39-40,

and note thereto.

17. An excellent analysis of the differences between the original of

Doidalsas, c. 250 B.C., and the Rhodian variant, c. 100 B.C., here

Pl. XII, bottom, appears in R. Lullies and M. Hirmer op. cit. 80, Pl. 257.

18. C. Brendel, "Weiblicher Torso in Oslo," Die Antike 6 (1930) 52, Figs. 5-6; G. Perrot, "Une statuette de la Cyrénaique et l'Aphrodite Anadyomene d'Apelle," MonPiot 13 (1906) 117-35, Pl. 10; now on loan to the University Museum, Philadelphia, from the collection of Mr. and Mrs. Beaumont W. Wright.

19. Encyclopédie photographique de l'art III (Paris 1938) 230A; E. Michon, "Nouvelles statuettes d'Aphrodite provenant de l'Égypte," MonPiot 21 (1913) 163-72, Pls. 16, 17.

20. On the sandalbinder, supra, note 16; the dancer, D. Thompson, "A Bronze Dancer from Alexandria," AJA 54 (1950) 371-85, Figs. 1-17; the satyr, S. Aurigemma, The Baths of Diocletian and Museo Nazionale Romano (Rome 1947) 37, no. 499, Pl. 38a.  The under life-size type of the satyr twisting on axis to inspect his tail is cited as typical of mid-third century B.C. by R. Lullies in "Statuette einer Tänzerin," Studies Presented to David Moore Robinson on his Seventieth Birthday, G. Mylonas, ed. (2 vols. St. Louis, Mo. 1951) I, 671-72, Pl. 70, but it is more typical of c. 210-200 B.C.  See D. von Bothmer, Greek, Etruscan and Roman Antiquities, an Exhibition from the Collection of Walter Cummings Baker, Esq. (New York 1950) 9, no. 45, with illustration; Ancient Art in American Private Collections, a Loan Exhibition at the Fogg Art Museum of Harvard University (Cambridge 1954) 32, no. 222, Pl. 68, both showing a figure of Hypnos(?) whose composition is characteristic of the late third century B.C.

21. C. Edgar, Catalogue général des antiquités égyptiennes du Musée du Caire IV: Greek Sculpture (Cairo 1903) 11-12, nos. 27454-56, Pl. 6; L. Caskey, Museum of Fine Arts, Boston: Catalogue of Greek and Roman Sculpture (Cambridge [Mass.] 1925) 173, no. 96, cf. 172, no. 95; E. Michon loc. cit.; J. Charbonneaux, Les terres cuites grecques (Paris 1936) 20, 74, Pl. 81.

22. C. Edgar loc. cit.

23. G. Richter, Three Critical Periods (1951) 27-33, takes what is perhaps too internationalist a position. The emphasis upon separate schools belongs to the previous phase of scholarship in the Hellenistic field; see the rigid divisions in G. Dickins, Hellenistic Sculpture (Oxford 1920). The turning point occurred in the 1920's with the studies of G. Krahmer, esp. his "Stilphasen der hellenistischen Plastik,' RM 38-39 (1923-24), and "Die einansichtige Gruppe und die spathellenistische Kunst," GöttNachr (1927) 53-91, which presupposed regular phases of formal development, embracing more than one region. Cf. A. Lawrence, Later Greek Sculpture and Its Influence on East and West (London 1927), preceded by his articles, "Rhodes and Hellenistic Sculpture," BSA 26 (1923-25) 67-71, Pls. 8-10, and "Greek Sculpture in Ptolemaic Egypt," JEA 11 (1925) 179-91, Pls. 18-21, who occupies a bifurcated position embracing both views.

# ABBREVIATIONS[#]

AA--Archäologischer Anzeiger

Abh. der sächs. Akad. der Wiss.--Abhandlungen der Sächsischen Akademie
  der Wissenschaften, Philologisch-Historische Klasse, Leipzig

AJA--American Journal of Archaeology

AM--Mitteilungen des Deutschen Archäologischen Instituts, Athenische
  Abteilung

AntCl--L'Antiquité classique

ArchCl--Archeologia Classica

ArtB--Art Bulletin

ArchErt--Archaeologiai Ertesitö

Arti Figurative--Arti Figurative, Rivista d'Arte, Antica e Moderna

ASAE--Annales du Service des antiquités de l'Égypte

ASAtene--Annuario della R. Scuola Archeologica di Atene

AZ--Archäologische Zeitung

BAntFr--Bulletin de la Société nationale des antiquaires de France

BCH--Bulletin de correspondance hellénique

BerlMus--Berliner Museen, Berichte aus den preussischen Kunstsammlungen

BMCC--British Museum Catalogue of Coins

BMMA--Bulletin of the Metropolitan Museum of Art, New York

----

#NOTE: The abbreviations for classical authors and their works
follow those given in OCD, ix-xix.

BrBr--Brunn-Bruckmann, Denkmäler griechischer und römischer Skulptur, continued by Arndt-Lippold, Munich, 1888-1947

BSA--British School at Athens, Annual

BSRAA--Bulletin de la Société r. d'archéologie d'Alexandrie

BullComm--Bullettino della Commissione Archeologica Comunale di Roma

Burl. Magaz.--Burlington Magazine for Connoisseurs

ClRhod--Clara Rhodos. Istituto Storico Archeologico di Rodi

EA--Photographische Einzelaufnahmen antiker Skulpturen. P. Arndt and W. Amelung, et al. eds. Munich 1893-

Ency. Brit.--Encyclopedia Britannica

Encyclopédie photographique III--Encyclopédie photographique de l'art III: Grèce et Rome. Eds. TEL, Paris, 1938

FuF--Forschungen und Fortschritte

GBA--Gazette des beaux-arts

GöttNachr--Nachrichten von der Gesellschaft der Wissenschaften zu Göttingen

HThR--Harvard Theological Review

JdI--Jahrbuch des k. deutschen archäologischen Instituts

JEA--Journal of Egyptian Archaeology

JHS--Journal of Hellenic Studies

MAAR--Memoirs of the American Academy in Rome

MdI--Mitteilungen des deutschen archäologischen Instituts

MemPontAcc--Atti della Pontificia Accademia Romana di Archeologia, Memorie

MjB--Münchener Jahrbuch der bildenden Kunst

MonPiot--Monuments et mémoires publ. par l'Académie des inscriptions et
    belles lettres.  Fondation Piot

MusHelv--Museum Helveticum

NSc--Notizie degli Scavi di Antichità

OCD--Oxford Classical Dictionary.  M. Cary and A. D. Nock, et al., eds.
    Oxford, 1949

ProcPhilSoc--Proceedings of the American Philosophical Society

RA--Revue archéologique

RE--Pauly-Wissowa, Real-Encyclopädie der klassischen Altertumswissenschaft

Revue des Arts--La Revue des Arts

RevPhil--Revue de philologie, de littérature et d'histoire ancienne

RM--Mitteilungen des deutschen archäologischen Instituts, Römische
    Abteilung

SB--Sitzungsberichte...

Schriftquellen--Overbeck, J.  Die antiken Schriftquellen zur Geschichte
    der bildenden Künste bei den Griechen.  Leipzig, 1868.

SELECTED BIBLIOGRAPHY[#]

Abramíc, M. "Die 'asiatische Aphrodite' aus Virunum," Festschrift für
    Rudolf Egger; Beiträge zur älteren europäischen Kulturgeschichte.
    G. Moro, ed. Vol. III, Klagenfurt, 1954. 135-38.

Adriani, A. "L'Afrodite al bagno di Rodi e l'Afrodite di Doedalsas,"
    ASAE 44 (1944) 37-70.

_____ "Contributo allo studio dell 'Afrodite di Doedalsas," BSRAA
    39 (1951) 144-81.

Alexander, C. "A Statue of Aphrodite," BMMA 11 (1953) 241-51.

Alscher, L. Griechische Plastik III: Nachklassik und Vorhellenismus.
    Berlin, Veb deutscher Verlag der Wiss., 1956.

Anti, C. "Nuove repliche della Venere che si toglie il sandalo,"
    Bollettino del Museo Civico di Padova 20 (1927) 17-38.

_____ "La Venere 'Maliziosa' di Cirene," Daedalo 11 (1926) 683-701.

Bagnani, G. "Hellenistic Sculpture from Cyrene," JHS 41 (1921) 232-46.

Becatti, G. "Attika--Saggio sulla scultura attica dell'ellenismo,"
    RivIstArch 7 (1940) 7-116.

---

[#]NOTE: Dictionaries, excavation reports, museum catalogues, and
reference works are not included. The bibliography is limited to studies
pertinent to an understanding of the development of Hellenistic sculpture and statuary types of Aphrodite within that sequence.

_____ "Le tre grazie," BullComm 65 (1937) 41-60.

Benndorf, O. "Bemerkungen zur griechischen Kunstgeschichte III:
Anadyomene des Apelles," AM 1 (1876) 50-66.

Bernhart, M. Aphrodite auf griechischen Münzen: eine numismatische
Materialsammlung. Munich, Kress und Hornung, [1936].

Bernoulli, J. Aphrodite, ein Baustein zur griechischen Kunstmythologie.
Leipzig, Engelmann, 1873.

Bieber, M. The Sculpture of the Hellenistic Age. New York, Columbia
University Press, 1955.

_____ "Die Söhne des Praxiteles," JdI 38-39 (1923-24) 242-75.

_____ "Späthellenistische Frauenstatuen aus Kos," Antike Plastik,
W. Amelung zum 60. Geburtstag. Berlin and Leipzig, de Gruyter,
1928. 16-23.

_____ "Die Venus Genetrix des Arkesilaos," RM 48 (1933) 261-276.

Brendel, O. "Weiblicher Torso in Oslo," Die Antike 6 (1930) 41-64.

Broneer, O. "The Armed Aphrodite on Acrocorinth and the Aphrodite of
Capua," University of California Publications in Classical Archaeology I. Berkeley, University of California Press, 1930. 65-84.

Bulard, M. "Aphrodite. Pan et Éros," BCH 30 (1906) 610-31.

Burr, D. Terra-Cottas from Myrina in the Museum of Fine Arts, Boston.
Vienna, A. Holzhausens Nachfolger, 1934.

Byvanck, A. "La chronologie de Praxitèle," Mnemosyne 4 (1951) 204-15.

Carpenter, R. "Observations on Familiar Statuary in Rome," MAAR 18 (1941).

Charbonneaux, J. "L'Aphrodite de Cnide de la collection Kaufmann,"
Revue des Arts 3 (1951) 174-76.

_____ "Le geste de la Vénus de Milo," Revue des Arts 6 (1956) 105-06.

_____ Les terres cultes grecques. Paris, L. Reynaud, 1936.

_____ "La Vénus de Milo et Mithridate le Grand," Revue des Arts 1 (1951) 8-16.

Clark, K. The Nude: A Study in Ideal Form. The A. W. Mellon Lectures in the Fine Arts, 1953, National Gallery of Art, Washington; Bollingen Series 36, 2. New York, Pantheon, 1956.

Curtius, L. "Die Aphrodite von Kyrene," Die Antike 1 (1925) 36-60.

Deonna, W. "Aphrodite a la coquille," RA 6 (1917) 392-416.

_____ "Le groupe des trois graces nues et sa descendance," RA 31 (1930) 274-332.

Deubner, O. Hellenistische Apollogestalten. Munich, Ph.D. Dissertation, 1934.

Dickins, G. "The Followers of Praxiteles," BSA 21 (1914-15) 1-10.

_____ Hellenistic Sculpture. Oxford, Clarendon Press, 1920.

Felletti-Maj, B. "Afrodite pudica: Saggio d'arte ellenistica," ArchCl 3 (1951) 33-65.

Fredrich, C. "Die Aphrodite von Aphrodisias in Karien," AM 22 (1897) 361-80.

Fuchs, W. "Zum Aphrodite-Typus Louvre-Neapel und seiner neuattischen Umbildungen," Neue Beiträge zur klassischen Altertumswissenschaft: Festschrift zum 60. Geburtstag von B. Schweitzer. R. Lullies, ed. Stuttgart and Cologne, Kohlhammer, 1954. 206-17.

Furtwängler, A. "Aphrodite Diadumene und Anadyomene," (Helbings) Monatsberichte über Kunstwissenschaft und Kunsthandel 1 (1901) 177-81.

_____ Masterpieces of Greek Sculpture. E. Sellers, ed. London, Heinemann, 1895.

Giuliano, A. "La Afrodite Callipige di Siracusa," ArchCl 5 (1953) 210-14.

Goetz, H. "Aphrodite Urania: An Asiatic Cult in Ancient Greece, and a Corinthian Bronze in the Baroda Museum," Bulletin of the Baroda State Museum and Picture Gallery 3 (1946) 1-15.

Gullini, G. "Su alcune sculture del tardo Ellenismo," Arti Figurative 3 (1947) 61-72.

Himmelmann-Wildschutz, N. "Zur knidischen Aphrodite I," Marburger Winckelmann-Programm (1957) 11-16.

Horn, R. "Stehende weibliche Gewandstatuen in der hellenistischen Plastik," RM Ergänzungsheft 2 (1931).

_____ "Hellenistische Köpfe," RM 53 (1938) 70-90.

Jacobi, G. "L'Afrodite Pudica del Museo Archeologico di Rodi," BdA 9 (1929-30) 401-09.

Klein, W. Praxiteles. Leipzig, Veit & Co., 1898.

_____ Vom antiken Rokoko. Vienna, Hölzel & Co., 1921.

Kleiner, G. "Tanagrafiguren: Untersuchungen zur hellenistischen Kunst und Geschichte," JdI Ergänzungsheft 15 (1942).

Krahmer, G. "Hellenisztikus Léany-Szobrocska Budapesten," ArchErt 41 (1927) 1-30.

_____ "Stilphasen der hellenistischen Plastik," RM 38-39 (1923-24) 138-84.

Lawrence, A. "Cessavit ars: Turning Points in Hellenistic Sculpture,"
Mélanges C. Picard, vol. 2 RA 31-32, (1948) 581-86.

———— "Greek Sculpture in Ptolemaic Egypt," JEA 11 (1925) 179-91.

———— Later Greek Sculpture and Its Influence on East and West.
New York, Harcourt, Brace, 1927.

Laurenzi, L. "Lineamenti d'arte ellenistica," Arti Figurative 1 (1945)
13-28.

———— "Rilievi e statue d'arte Rodia," RM 54, (1939) 42-65.

———— "Sculture inedite del Museo di Coo," ASAtene 17-18 (1955-56)
59-156.

Lévêque, P. "Notes de sculpture rhodienne (II)," BCH 74 (1950) 62-69.

Lippold, G. Die griechische Plastik. Munich, 1950. V, vol. III, bk. 1
of Handbuch der Archaeologie. W. Otto and R. Herbig, eds. 6 parts,
Munich 1937-53.

———— Kopien und Umbildungen griechischer Statuen. Munich, C. Beck,
1923.

Lullies, R. Die kauernde Aphrodite. Munich-Pasing, Filser Verlag, 1954.

———— "Statuette einer Tänzerin," Studies Presented to D. M. Robinson on his Seventieth Birthday. G. Mylonas, ed. Two vols. St.
Louis, Washington University, 1951-53. Vol. 1, 668-73.

———— "Zum Motiv der kauernde Aphrodite," FuF 21 (1947) 136-38.

———— "Zur drei-Grazien-Gruppe,' MdI 1 (1948) 45-52.

Macurdy, G. Hellenistic Queens. The Johns Hopkins Studies in Archaeology, No. 14. Baltimore, The Johns Hopkins Press, 1932.

Marconi, G. "Gruppi erotici dell'ellenismo nei musei di Roma," BullComm 41 (1924) 225-98.

Mariani, L. "L'Afrodite di Cirene," BdA 8 (1914) 177-84.

Miro, E. de. "Statuette di Afrodite accoccolata al Museo di Agrigento," ArchCl 8 (1956) 48-52.

Mot, J. de. "L'Aphrodite d'Arenberg," RA 2 (1903) 10-20.

Muller, V. "A Chronology of Greek Sculpture, 400-40 B.C.," ArtB 20 (1938) 359-418.

Noshy, I. The Arts in Ptolemaic Egypt: A Study of Greek and Egyptian Influences in Ptolemaic Architecture and Sculpture. Oxford, Clarendon Press, 1937.

Perrot, G. "Une statuette de la Cyrénaique et l'Aphrodite Anadyomene d'Apelle," MonPiot 13 (1906) 117-35.

Pesce, G. L"Afrodite da Sinvessa. R. Istituto d'archeologia e storia dell'arte, Fasc. 9. Rome, Istituto poligrafico dello stato, libreria dello stato, 1939.

Pfuhl, E. "Ikonographische Beiträge zur Stilgeschichte der hellenistischen Kunst," JdI 45 (1930) 1-61.

Picard, C. Manuel d'archéologie grecque. Paris, E. Picard, 1935-1954. 4 vols. (Manuels d'archéologie et d'histoire de l'art). Vol. III: La sculpture, période classique--IVe siècle, Vol. IV: La sculpture, période classique--IVe siècle, pt. 2.

Pliny, trans. K. Jex-Blake and E. Sellers. The Elder Pliny's Chapters on the History of Art. London, MacMillan, 1896.

Poulsen, F. "Gab es eine alexandrinische Kunst?" From the Collections

of the Ny Carlsberg Glyptothek. Vol. II. Copenhagen, 1938, 1-52.

_____ "Sur la Pséliuméné de Praxitèle," RA 9 (1907) 69-74.

Reinach, S. "Un indice chronologique applicable aux figures féminines

de l'art grec," Revue des Études grecques 21 (1908) 13-38.

_____ "Statuette d Aphrodite découverte dans la basse Égypte," RA

3 (1904) 374-81.

_____ "La Vénus d'Alesia," ProAlesia 1 (1906) 65-71.

Reinach, T. "L'Auteur de la'Vénus accroupie,'" GBA 17 (1897) 314-22.

Ricci, S. de. "Groupe en marbre de la collection Dattari," RA 10 (1907)

103-07.

Richer, P. Le Nu dans l'art: vol. 2, l'art grec. Paris, Les petits-

fils de Plonet Nourrit, 1926.

Richter, G. M. A. Three Critical Periods in Greek Sculpture. Oxford,

Clarendon Press, 1951.

_____ "Two Bronze Statuettes," AJA 37 (1933) 48-51.

_____ The Sculpture and Sculptors of the Greeks. Rev. ed., New

Haven, Yale University Press, 1950.

Rizzo, G. E. Prassitele. Milan and Rome, Fratelli Treves, 1932.

Schefold, K. Kertscher Vasen. Part 3 of Bilder griechischer Vasen,

Beazley-Jacobsthal ed. Berlin-Wilmersdorf, H. Keller, 1930.

_____ Untersuchungen zu den Kertscher Vasen. Vol. IV of Archäolo-

gische Mitteilungen aus russischen Sammlungen. Berlin and Leipzig,

de Gruyter, 1934.

Schmidt, E. "Ueber einige Fälle der Uebertragung gemalter Figuren in Rundplastik," Festschrift fur P. Arndt. Munich, Bruckmann, 1925. 96-114.

Schweitzer, B. Xenokrates von Athen. Book 3 of Schriften der Königsberger Gelehrten Gesellschaft, Geisteswissenschaftliche Klasse. Halle (Saale), Niemeyer, 1932.

Stark, K. "Ueber unedierte Venusstatuen und das Venusideal seit Praxiteles," Berichte der Sächsischen Gesellschaft der Wissenschaft (1860) 46-97.

Süsserott, H. Griechische Plastik des vierten Jahrhunderts vor Christus: Untersuchungen zur Zeitbestimmung. Frankfurt-am-Main, Klosterman, 1938.

Swindler, M. "Venus Pompeiiana and the New Pompeiian Frescoes," AJA 27 (1923) 302-13.

Thompson, D. "A Bronze Dancer from Alexandria," AJA 54 (1950) 371-85.
_____ "Three Centuries of Hellenistic Terracottas, II, The Early Third Century B.C.," Hesperia 26 (1957) 108-28.

Visscher, F. de, Ruyt, F. de, De Laet, S. J. and Hertens, J. "Les fouilles d'Alba Fucens (Italie Centrale) de 1951 à 1953," AntCl 24 (1955) 51-119.

Vita, de A. "L'Afrodite pudica da Punta delle Sabbie," ArchCl 7 (1955) 9-23.

Waddington, W. H., Babelon, E., and Reinach, T. Recueil général des monnaies grecques d'Asie Mineure. Tome-1, fascicules 1-4, Académie des inscriptions et belles lettres (Fondation Piot). Paris, E. Leroux, 1904-12.

Winter, F.  Die Typen der figürlichen Terrakotten.  Vol. III, pt. 2 of

    Die antiken Terrakotten.  Berlin, Spemann, 1903.

Zschietzschmann, W.  Die hellenistische und römische Kunst.  Pt. 2 of

    Die antike Kunst, and vol. II, pt. 2 of Handbuch der Kunstwissen-

    schaft, E. A. Brinckmann, ed.  Potsdam, Akademische Verlagsgesell-

    schaft Athenaion, 1939.

PLATES

PLATE I.   APHRODITE OF ARLES

Left:   UNRESTORED, FROM CAST.  Museum, Arles

Right:  THE RESTORED FIGURE.  Louvre, Paris

PLATE II.   ADAPTATION OF THE APHRODITE OF CNIDOS

Metropolitan Museum of Art, New York

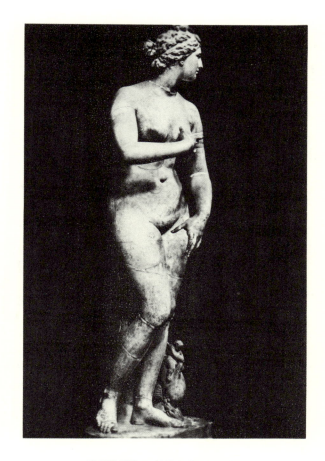

PLATE III.  APHRODITE MEDICI

Uffizi Gallery, Florence

PLATE IV.  TYCHE OF ANTIOCH

Metropolitan Museum of Art, New York

PLATE V.  SEATED HERMES

Metropolitan Museum of Art, New York

PLATE VI.  APHRODITE, FRONT VIEW

Museum of Art, R. I. School of Design, Providence

PLATE VII.  APHRODITE, BACK VIEW

Museum of Art, R. I. School of Design, Providence

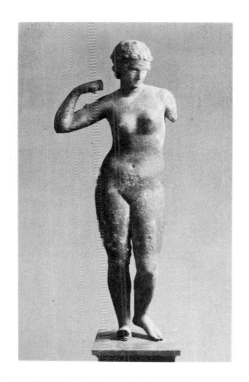

PLATE VIII.  WOMAN PUTTING ON A STEPHANE

Metropolitan Museum of Art, New York

PLATE IX.   CROUCHING APHRODITE, FROM HADRIAN'S VILLA

Museo Nazionale Romano, Rome

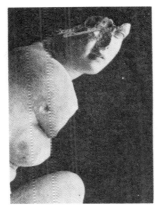

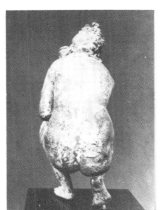

PLATE X.  CROUCHING APHRODITE

Top:     HEAD OF STATUE FROM TIVOLI, THREE VIEWS

        Museo Nazionale Romano, Rome

Bottom:  STATUETTE FROM ROME, THREE VIEWS

        Ny Carlsberg Glyptothek, Copenhagen

PLATE XI.  APHRODITE PUTTING ON A NECKLACE

British Museum, London

PLATE XII.   EARLY AND LATE HELLENISTIC STATUES OF APHRODITE

Top:      APHRODITE PUTTING ON A NECKLACE

          British Museum, London

Bottom:   CROUCHING APHRODITE, FROM RHODES

          Museum, Rhodes

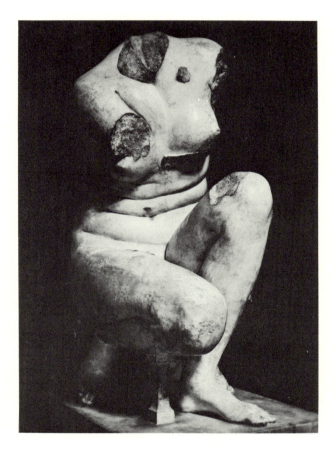

PLATE XIII.   CROUCHING APHRODITE, FROM VIENNE

Louvre, Paris

PLATE XIV.  APHRODITE BINDING HER SANDAL, FROM PATRAS

British Museum, London

PLATE XV.   APHRODITE BINDING HER SANDAL, FROM PARAMYTHIA

British Museum, London

PLATE XVI. APHRODITE BINDING HER SANDAL, FROM PADUA,

FRONT VIEW        Museo Civico, Padua

PLATE XVII.  APHRODITE BINDING HER SANDAL, FROM PADUA,

SIDE VIEW    Museo Civico, Padua

PLATE XVIII. APHRODITE BINDING HER SANDAL

British Museum, London

PLATE XIX.  HERMES BINDING HIS SANDAL

Ny Carlsberg Glyptothek, Copenhagen

PLATE XX.   HEAD OF ARSINOË III

Palazzo Ducale, Mantua

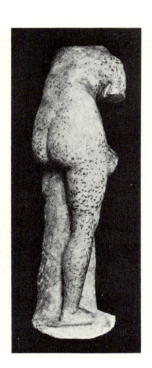

PLATE XXI.   APHRODITE BINDING HER SANDAL, FROM EGYPT

THREE VIEWS.   Palais Arenberg, Brussels

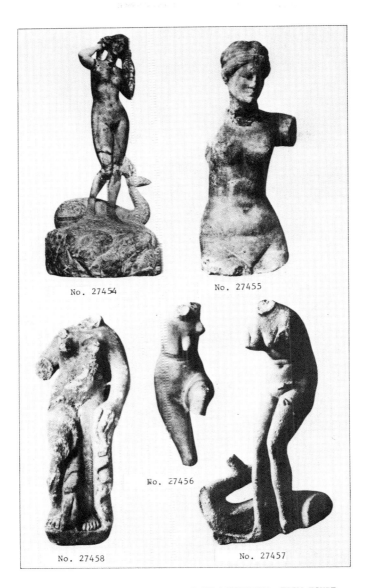

No. 27454

No. 27455

No. 27456

No. 27458

No. 27457

PLATE XXII.  VARIOUS STATUES OF APHRODITE, FROM EGYPT

No. 27454:  APHRODITE ANADYOMENE

No. 27455:  HEAD AND TORSO OF APHRODITE

No. 27456:  TORSO OF APHRODITE BINDING HER SANDAL

No. 27457:  ADAPTATION OF THE APHRODITE OF CNIDOS

No. 27458:  SEATED APHRODITE, HEADLESS

Museum, Cairo

PLATE XXIII.   APHRODITE BINDING HER SANDAL

Altes Museum, Berlin

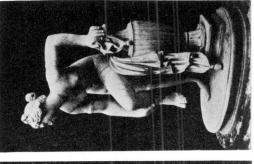

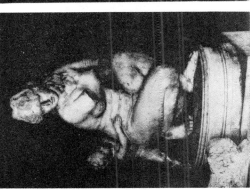

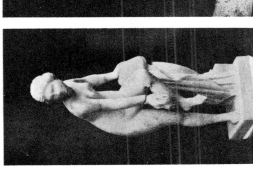

PLATE XXIV. APHRODITE STATUES. Once in Cook Coll., London

Left: BINDING SANDAL, RESTORED AS WASHING HER FEET

Center: CROUCHING, WITH EROS. Getty Mus., Malibu, Calif.

Right: BINDING SANDAL

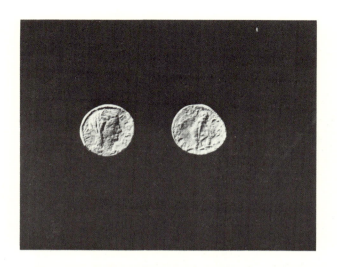

PLATE XXV.   DRACHMS OF APHRODISIAS IN CARIA

Top:    Obverse - HEAD OF BOULE

        Reverse - APHRODITE BINDING HER SANDAL

Bottom:  Obverse - HEAD OF COMMODUS

        Reverse - CULT IMAGE OF APHRODITE IN TEMPLE

Museum of the American Numismatic Society, New York

8245

PLATE XXVI. APHRODITE BENDING HER SANDAL, FROM SMYRNA

Terra Cotta, Museum of Fine Arts, Boston

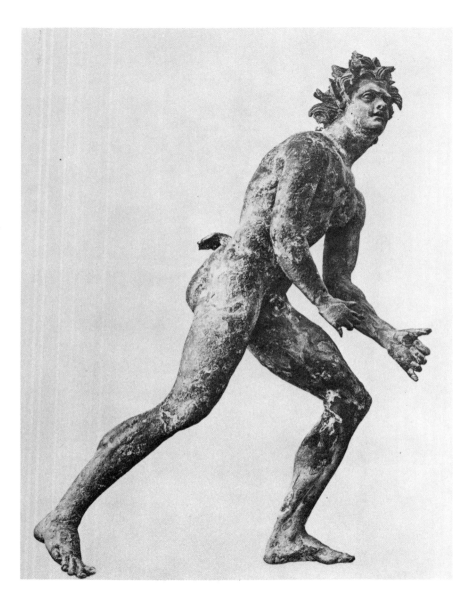

PLATE XXVII.  SATYR

Bardo, Tunis

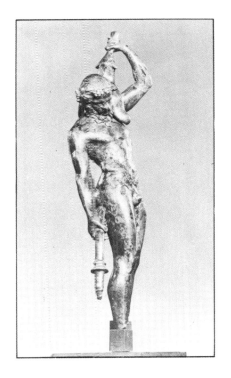

PLATE XXVIII.   SATYR WITH TORCH

Metropolitan Museum of Art, New York

PLATE XXIX.   DANCING SATYR

Metropolitan Museum of Art, New York

PLATE XXX.   SATYR AND NYMPH GROUP, RECONSTRUCTION

Once at the University of Prague

PLATE XXXI.   SATYR AND NYMPH GROUP, RECONSTRUCTION

Once at the University of Prague

PLATE XXXII.  HEAD OF SATYR FROM SATYR AND NYMPH GROUP

Museo Archæologico, Venice

PLATE XXXIII.  HEAD OF NYMPH FROM SATYR AND NYMPH GROUP

Museo Archeologico, Venice

PLATE XXXIV.   HEAD OF NYMPH FROM SATYR AND NYMPH GROUP

Museo Archeologico, Venice

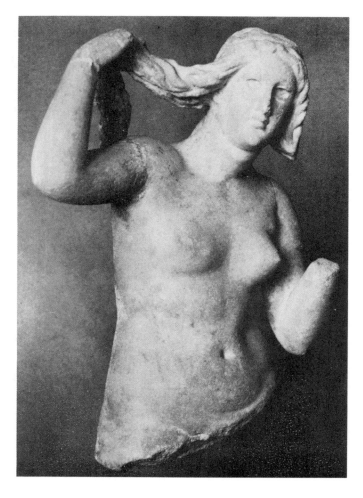

PLATE XXXV.  APHRODITE ANADYOMENE, FROM HORBEIT, EGYPT

Louvre, Paris

PLATE XXXVI.  CAPITOLINE APHRODITE

Museo Capitolino, Rome

PLATE XXXVII.  APHRODITE UNDRESSING, FROM EGYPT

Louvre, Paris

PLATE XXXVIII.   HALF-DRAPED APHRODITE FROM RHODES

Fogg Art Museum, Harvard University, Cambridge, Massachusetts

PLATE XXXIX.   FEMALE FIGURE, POSSIBLY APHRODITE

Worcester Art Museum, Worcester, Massachusetts

PLATE XL.   HALF-DRAPED APHRODITE ANADYOMENE

Museo Vaticano, Rome

PLATE XLI.   APHRODITE ANADYOMENE

Metropolitan Museum of Art, New York

PLATE XLII.   APHRODITE

Museo Vaticano, Rome

PLATE XLIII.  APHRODITE ANADYOMENE, FROM CYRENE

FRONT VIEW.  Museo Nazionale Romano, Rome

PLATE XLIV.  APHRODITE ANADYOMENE, FROM CYRENE

BACK VIEW.  Museo Nazionale Romano, Rome

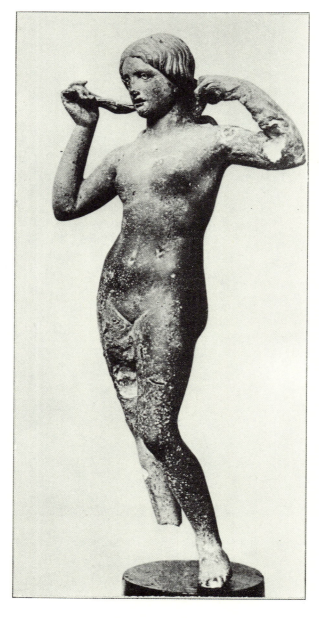

PLATE XLV. APHRODITE ANADYOMENE, FROM COURTRAI

Musée de Mariemont, Mariemont, Belgium

PLATE XLVI.  APHRODITE ANADYOMENE, FROM MADYOS

Terra-Cotta, Once Coll. Loeb, Munich

PLATE XLVII.  MOULD OF APHRODITE ANADYOMENE, FROM EGYPT

Museum, Cairo

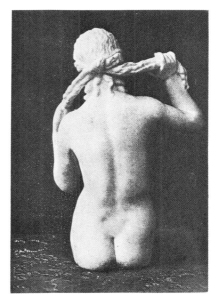

PLATE XLVIII.  APHRODITE ANADYOMENE, FROM CYRENAICA

Coll. Wright, on loan to University Museum, Philadelphia

PLATE XLIX.  APHRODITE ANADYOMENE, WITH EROS

Terra-Cotta, Walters Art Gallery, Baltimore

PLATE L.   EXAMPLES OF APHRODITE ANADYOMENE OF ROMAN DATE

    <u>Top</u>   :  NUDE TYPE, FROM BATHS OF CARACALLA

           Museo Nazionale Romano, Rome

    <u>Bottom</u>:  HALF-DRAPED TYPE, FROM SINUESSA

           Museo Nazionale, Naples

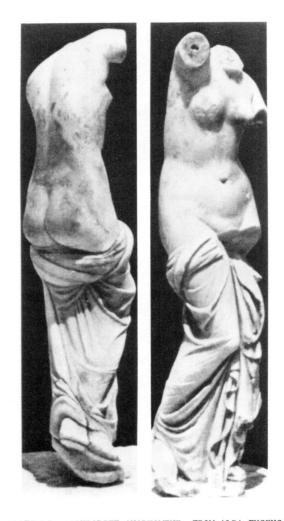

PLATE LI.   APHRODITE ANADYOMENE, FROM ALBA FUCENS

Museo Nazionale Romano, Rome

PLATE LII.  APHRODITE, FROM MELOS

Louvre, Paris